Praise for *Paradoxia*

MW01076500

"Lunch's headlong plunge into manic devastation and ~~~ times recalls the better work of William S. Burroughs . . . Strangely honest rantings from a modern-day Genet."

—*Kirkus Reviews*

"A lurid, profane account of downtown living . . ."

—*Newsday*, "Our Favorites of 2007"

"Beyond the book's chronicling of Lunch's desires, it serves an over-arching, exhibitionist desire to perform, and it brings a decrepit, vanished New York to life . . . It recreates its time and place with vivid authenticity."

—*Publishers Weekly*

"*Paradoxia* is compelling, exhilarating, and infinitely readable."

—*Paper*

"*Paradoxia* is very much a cultural document—a glimpse of the warts-and-all attitude of someone who strove to be transgressive and often succeeded. Through streaming open-mike cadences, staccato scorn, and a highly attuned olfactory memory, Lunch captures the swoony, viscous downtown of yesteryear, when sex and the city meant something else entirely."

—*Time Out New York* (4 stars)

"Hubert Selby, Jr. famously said that he grew up feeling like a scream without a mouth. Lydia Lunch, one of his most celebrated—and most uncompromising—literary progeny, delivered scream, mouth, teeth, blood, hair, sperm, knife, and adrenaline in her purgatorial masterpiece *Paradoxia*."

—Jerry Stahl, author of *Permanent Midnight*

"Intoxicating. Dirty. Erotic. Damn, Lydia Lunch's *Paradoxia* intrigues and resonates with every word . . . [It] is a seductive and redemptive story of lust—lust for satisfaction, for power, for solitude, and for understanding how to live."

—*Feminist Review*

"*Paradoxia* reveals that Lunch is at her best when she's at her worst . . . and gives voice to her sometimes scary, frequently funny, always canny, never sentimental siren song."
—Barbara Kruger, *Artforum*

"A gritty, autobiographical tale of hedonistic excess through three decades."
—*Los Angeles Times*

"[*Paradoxia*] is real noir in a declamatory and clear voice . . . In a culture where the 'true' has been denatured, Lunch reclaims its bestial power."
—*Eye Weekly* (Toronto)

"Lydia Lunch often is compared to Hubert Selby, Jr. and Jean Genet. Reading *Paradoxia*, I see some Dostoevsky in her shattered protagonist and her unforgettable, murderous opening line . . . *Paradoxia* has a place in the literature of depravity, and like the good work in that genre, it's intentionally funny."
—*Bookslut*

"Within the body of her blunt bullet point prose . . . Lunch can be brutally original. Or originally brutal."
—*Harp*

"*Paradoxia* is at once a moving confessional of an irredeemably abused girl and a steely-eyed account of that girl's coming to womanhood by meticulously, soberly reclaiming that abuse."
—*Bust*

"Lunch's direct and visceral prose and her skill in shaping exciting narratives make *Paradoxia* a compelling page-turner."
—*Hipster Book Club*

WILL
WORK
FOR
DRUGS

WILL
WORK
FOR
DRUGS

by LYDIA LUNCH

with a foreword by Karen Finley

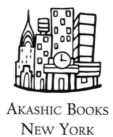

AKASHIC BOOKS
NEW YORK

All rights reserved. No part of this book may be used or reproduced in any manner whatsoever without the written permission of the publisher.

Published by Akashic Books
©2009 by Lydia Lunch
Foreword ©2009 by Karen Finley

ISBN-13: 978-1-933354-73-6
Library of Congress Control Number: 2008937351

First printing

Some of the stories in this volume originally appeared in an earlier form in the following publications: *Sex and Guts*: "Death Defied by a Thousand Cuts"; *The Wire*: "1967"; *Inappropriate Behavior: Prada Sucks! and other Demented Descants* edited by Jessica Berens and Kerri Sharp (Serpent's Tail, 2002): "Motherhood: It's Not Compulsory"; *Your Flesh Magazine*: "Assume the Position"; *Another Man Magazine*: "'In Times of Universal Deceit . . .'"; *Incriminating Evidence* by Lydia Lunch (Last Gasp, 1992): "The Beast"; *Storie*: "Johnny behind the Deuce"; *Dirt*: "Hubert Selby Jr.: The Man Who Refused to Die"; *Sex and Guts*: "Nick Tosches: Squalor and Splendor"; *Crave*: "Jerry Stahl: The Living Perv"; *Sex and Guts*: "The Violent Disbelief of Ron Athey."

Akashic Books
PO Box 1456
New York, NY 10009
info@akashicbooks.com
www.akashicbooks.com

TABLE OF CONTENTS

FOREWORD

BY KAREN FINLEY

Lydia Lunch is a contemporary renaissance poetess, musician, artist, and provocateur. Her career has spanned three decades and has influenced a range of styles and content, through genres of music, spoken word, performance, film, gender and sexuality, humor and politics. She is also a cultural critic and has been a major pioneer in the international art scene. One of Lydia's most powerful contributions to the art world has been her unique skill at transforming her traumatic childhood ordeals into daring and illuminating expressions that enforce and inspire creative responses rather than eliciting destructive ones.

In this collection of personal essays, short fiction, and interviews, Lydia presents her own life for reflection to once and for all void the diary as a self-indulgent exercise or tool of pity. Her generosity with her own life experiences provides the reader an opportunity to glimpse the creative potential as outlet. Alice Miller writes about the relationship of trauma and the imagination in *The Drama of the Gifted Child*. And here, in *Will Work for Drugs*, Lydia gives evidence of redirecting her traumas by how she escapes through the lens of the imagination. We enter her commitment to (and love of) the imagination, and exit with the knowledge of the power of that creative sphere.

Lydia refuses to be subservient to the destructive acts she has witnessed, and instead develops sacred space in the intimacy of this book and nurtures the *collective* sacred space with the activation of her life as art, her words and deeds as the illumination of art.

When in doubt, her faith kicks in and she continues creating, transforming—despite the odds and circumstances—amidst the fragility of human existence. Lydia survives with swift humor which uncomfortably wraps and soothes the anger with a bitchy wit and sardonic word-tailoring that continues a long tradition of jester, comedienne, and political humorist.

Although her point of departure is usually the experience of self, she maps her territory for us as a community organizer for the disenfranchised. Lydia positions herself as an outside/inside agitator, inciting to chaos, breaking the depressive calm as she threatens the community to wake up and take action. Wear and utilize your emotional soul burden as artistic pride.

At times we see her analyze—and reanalyze—historical and emotional events with intellectual passion and rigor while she deconstructs theories of complacency and political ideologies. She plays a cat-and-mouse game in her skill as a master debater. The cat never lets up. But she will let the mouse roar.

Lydia volunteers her own emotional life to become our mirror, to judge and learn from, laugh from; and then we can gaze upon our own hearts and heads. This generosity mesmerizes me, for Lydia does it with her twinkling assertive *je m'en fous*, *joie de vivre*, and heavy breathing. Her insistence on our acceptance of her gift is probably the only authentically aggressive part of her. If we don't see or hear her words, the now of emotional destruction is within reach.

Lydia presents the symbols and standards of power such as obedience, rules, punishment, and authority as true myths of the American Dream. She allows us a viewing from the underbelly, the shadow of our American life—or, rather, the American Nightmare. We understand our own versions and boundaries of morality. Lydia creates for us a disturbance by giving us her truth, though not with scientific methods. Consider, for example, her essay "1967," in which the outside political authority and the father authority break down and abuse their pathetic power over her.

Her courage—to be Lydia, to find Lydia, and to express Lydia—is the spiritual centerpiece and moral of the story. Through trial and error, she believes, the great human insistence of soul will eventually become an individuated self that will heal and give sustenance, guidance for those beginning the journey. The courage to not just witness but to take action with authority is an expression of love, beauty, truth, grace, and sensitivity—the stuff real art is made from. Lydia offers rage with attendant tenderness to the gentle palms holding her book, to the personal encounter of reading. *Will Work for Drugs* provides the soul search in the written word. What nurtures the soul of the artist? With Lydia Lunch it would never be the complacency of good intentions, or the inaction of thought and deeds.

It is a privilege and honor to introduce you to Lydia Lunch's *Will Work for Drugs*. I am certain you will be enthralled, moved, and riveted as you turn these pages written by one of America's National Treasures. You are in for quite a ride!

Karen Finley
March 2009

INTRODUCTION
WILL WORK FOR DRUGS

Yeah, right. I wish they made enough good drugs to reward the blood and brain matter I have splattered over these pages, countless stages, celluloid, vinyl, acetate, and compact disc. The fuel that propels me is more likely to be a grotesque imbalance of testosterone and estrogen polluted by multiple dioxins conveniently dumped in the Love Canal near Niagara Falls by the Hooker Chemical and Plastics Corporation for decades before my birth in Upstate New York.

It takes a master alchemist to create a functional stability between the contamination of genetic mutation, environmental hazards, moral pollution, hormonal imbalance, and toxic emotions from which I struggle. My daily existence is a battlecade of extreme fluctuations where chaos clobbers apathy which beats the shit out of depression which follows irritability which slams into anger which eclipses ecstasy which slips through my fingers far too often. I'm still searching for the drug that can trigger the switch which will allow euphoria its rightful position as a top contender in the war of my emotions.

I had my first mood swing while still in the womb when the the bliss of non-being was shattered by the bullrun of my father's bloodline brutally crashing through my fragile endocranial cast. The inside of my head has been punching the shit out of itself since I was a child. Migraines rebel against my internal landscape, that sewer of muscle, meat, sinew, and blood which stinks of sulfur and rose water. My brainpan overflows with ancient memories which have fractured into splintered obsidian only to be melted into tiny hammers whose thunder eventually roars out of my mouth. This collection commits to the page a sampling of the cries and whispers which batter the inside of my head like fevered ghosts ghoulishly intoxicated by the primordial essence which has poisoned my very existence. Enjoy—

Lydia Lunch
April 2009

PART I

DESPERATE MEASURES

DEATH DEFIED
BY A THOUSAND CUTS

I was born surrounded by Death. My mother miscarried before me, after me, and I was born choking the life out of my dead twin brother. At the age of six my grandmother, a cruel Sicilian witch with long white hair which smelled of camphor, died in bed while sleeping beside me. For years afterwards I was chased through the fruit cellar by the evil echo of her heinous cackle. My mother was surrounded by Death too: eleven brothers and sisters, only three of whom lived to see adulthood. Pneumonia. Tuberculosis. Cancer. Diabetes. Stroke. A sick brood indeed.

I spent my formative years in the town where future Hillside Strangler Kenneth Bianchi conducted his first experiments in lust killing. Month after month the lurid details of his latest victim, always a preadolescent girl my age, would be splayed across the evening news or the front page of the daily paper, grid-marking the map of bodies I was convinced I was next to join. Years later I survived a cocaine-induced killing spree by satanic heartthrob Richard Ramirez, who must have gotten his psychic signals crossed when instead of sneaking into my bungalow for a few carefree hours of hard metal and soft flesh, took a left turn and missed my apartment by a mere three blocks. Although at the time, in the advanced stages of a sick addiction to adrenaline and the endless pull of Death's black magnetism, I felt as if I had already spent many a new moon subjugated to the Night Stalker's unique charisma. Ricky never knew me, but I felt as if we were dating.

By nature I am Death defiant. I have survived illnesses which have killed lesser mortals. Burst appendix; infected lymph nodes; E. coli; "unintended intra-operative awareness"—the result of an undetected and unwanted ectopic pregnancy which exploded, filling my body with pus and poisoned blood, causing me to black out until I woke up seizing with the unbearable horror of being paralyzed under a Russian surgeon's vicious butchery in a scuzzy community hospital in downtown Los Angeles, surrounded by blinding white light, which was, in fact, not *the light*, but the fluorescent overheads, which I floated eye level with while silently screeching and beseeching every god, goddess, and demon whom I thought worthy of summoning, as I begged for Death, begged for relief, begged to be set free from what I assumed was Hell's ultimate punishment: unrelenting physical pain. Not enough anesthesia will do that to a person.

I have been stabbed in the gut an eighth of an inch short of pancreatic poisoning. I have been forced into the desert by a Manson wannabe whose idea of "True Romance" was bloodstains in the sun-bleached sand. I have been bottled in the forehead with a Heineken with such brute force it broke. I spent a charming weekend with a sexy drifter who was arrested three days later and charged with cannibalism. I have been held hostage in snowy woods by a Robert Blake look-alike holding a sawed-off shotgun to my left temple demanding to be told horrible fairy tales detailing a dozen ways in which I would murder my sisters.

I bullied a junkie gunman to put his piece back in his pocket, turn around, walk away from me, and go shoot someone from his own neighborhood. I guilt-tripped a knife-wielding crack tweeker to head uptown where people were actually worth sticking up. I've been on two transatlantic flights which were stalled on European runways for hours while bomb-sniffing dogs were sent through the luggage hold to retrieve deadly explosives. And that was just the early '80s . . .

I taunted Death, and Death taunted back. But like a lover who sweet talks you with endless promises of fantastic potential but always comes up short in the pants, you eventually grow bored with possibility. And the attraction you once swooned with now sours and leaves you cold. Besides, Death is *forever* . . . Life . . . no matter how much you torture yourself or allow others to pick up the pillory and nail you to a post, is goddamn short. Shit . . . sea turtles live longer.

I'm grateful for every minute I'm still alive. I've been granted numerous stays of execution. I courted Death, who always wins in the end, but truly I wanted LIFE. In the Extreme. I needed experiences which would force me to truly appreciate *everything*. I wanted to take nothing for granted.

A friend once said, "Shut the fuck up. You've got it made . . . You've had everything you ever wanted. All the sex you could stomach, all the drugs you could consume, cool friends who worshipped you. What more do you want?" I was glutting on everything in a desperate attempt to feel something, anything. I wasn't born numb to life, but the trauma of birth, repeated exposure to the violence of alcoholism and the rage of its impotence, poverty, and night terrors had short-circuited my emotional hard drive before I even hit puberty. I fought long and hard to get sensation back.

And yeah, I'm a fucking contrarian—on one hand, I simply DON'T GIVE A FUCK. A self-centered alien femme-bot soldiering forward in spite of the imminent collapse of my own physical and mental well-being, chortling sadistically as the planet crumbles. On the other hand, I'm war torn, battle fatigued, and deeply wounded by humanity's ignorance, stupidity, and greed. My compassion is a driving force which insists I give voice to the murdered sons and battered daughters who are forever looking for love in all the wrong faces because they didn't know how to love themselves enough while hating everything and everyone else.

Most people suffer from having too much emotion. They obsess over minor imperfections, comparing themselves to unrealistic images perpetrated by a celebrity-driven media who value net worth over content or meaning. They panic in the face of disapproval or contradiction, fearing that if they disagree with the staus quo, the general consensus, or a lover's opinion of right and wrong, they will be abandoned and left to fight it out alone. Their insecurity is exaggerated by jealousy, which in turn fosters such a desperate need to be understood that they'll waste an exorbitant amount of time and energy pitching temper tantrums riddled with endless tirades berating friends and lovers *who just don't get it.* Energy and emotion which could and should be more fruitfully employed elsewhere, like in the written and spoken word, where if somebody doesn't want to hear it—they aren't forced to listen. And if they *don't get it*—tough shit.

NO ONE MADE YOU BUY THIS BOOK—YOU BOUGHT IT BECAUSE YOU NEED TO VENT SOME POISON TOO. And I hope in return it inspires you to scream—not in your lover's face—but into the bottomless void of the eternal night backlit on some shitty stage howling your guts out seeking purgation surrounded by a handful of hungry orphans desperate for the nourishment of creation's offal.

1967

Blood buckets down the undulating walls. Invisible fists rage with superhuman strength and hammer the door. The ancient wood frame buckles, crumples, and heaves. The empty nursery reverberates with the mournful howl of a pitiful infant who cannot be located. I'm sitting cross-legged on the floor clutching my throat, trembling. Dry mouthed. Unable to breathe. *The Haunting of Hill House* is the most terrifying movie I've ever seen. I'm eight years old.

A suffocating humidity saturates the night air. Static electricity vibrates the hair follicles. The low buzzing hum of the black-and-white Motorola is swallowed up in the wheezing yelp of a stray dog, which bellows like a town crier somewhere in someone's backyard. His harried yapping immediately mimicked and amplified by every mutt in the neighborhood in a round robin of barks and howls. A desperate warning cry which signals the coming maelstrom.

The atmosphere stiffens. The dogs retreat. Time bends. In a sudden explosion of white noise, hundreds of frenzied voices come shrieking out of nowhere. As if all Hell's fury in a sudden expulsion from middle earth materializes, compounding my terror.

Men, women, and children who have been hoisted upon the backs of older brothers, all shouting slogans in a demonic gospeled fervor. *Equal work! Equal pay! Say it loud! We're black and we're proud!*

The riots of '67 have detoured down Clifford Avenue and are stampeding directly in front of my house. Hammers, baseball bats, pipes, and bricks all employed in the demolition of cars, windows, storefronts. A hideous industrial opera of unbearable din. My father chain-smokes and paces. Unleashing a litany of curses. Punches the air in his best Marlon Brando as his station wagon crumbles under the endless battery of physical abuse. The ambulance and firetrucks barrel in, splitting the angry throng in two. Their sirens a deafening symphony which exaggerate the cacophony. Police helicopters circle the periphery. Giant mechanical insects whose diabolical hum blankets the shrill.

My fear is drowned in sound but reborn as joy in flames. The family car is set on fire. I start to laugh. Maniacally. To dance. To sing. *"Come on baby LIGHT my FIRE. Try to set the night on FIRE!!!!"* My father assumes I've lost my mind and against my insistent protest sends me to my room.

I skulk upstairs dejected. "Kind of a drag," mumbled under my breath. A noisy rebellion of violence. Clanging. Pounding. Exciting. And I'm locked out! I can't really comprehend what's happening, but it feels so right. I'm no longer frightened, I'm charged up! Zoning in to the collective urgency. The passion. Determination. I head to the attic, my hidden retreat. Turn on the radio. Top 40 in 1967 was insane. "White Rabbit," "7-Rooms of Gloom," "Funky Broadway," "The Hunter Gets Captured by the Game," "Are You Experienced?" Back to back. I had no idea what any of these songs were referencing. What they really meant. How subversive they really were.

I used the radio to disappear. To escape from my family. Enter another dimension. Melt inside a psychedelic sound stage which cascaded out through the airwaves filling my already fractured psyche with throbbing, slinky, funkified soul music, where soaring rhythms and strangled guitars took me out of myself and gave me goose bumps.

"*I break out . . . in a cold sweat*" stimulated me in ways I could only express by shaking my ass, flapping my arms, and stomping my feet. Jimmy Lee Johnson, the seven-year-old black boy next door, "Skinny Legs and All," had the entire James Brown drop-to-one-knee, use-his-sweatshirt-as-a-cape routine down pat. It's the first time anyone flirted with me. I was amazed by his mimicry. His fluidity. His tiny body gliding through the air with so much passion and control. He must have caught JB on *The Ed Sullivan Show*. Everybody was glued to the tube on Sunday nights. The Rolling Stones, The Animals, George Carlin—all penetrated my unformed psyche, courtesy of Mr. Sullivan. Even the infamous Doors controversy where Morrison refused to change "*Girl, we couldn't get much higher,*" subsequently banning him from future appearances, struck a raw nerve in my adolescent conscience.

Music is the connective tissue between protest, rebellion, violence, sexual awareness, and community. Just the way it is. The Summer of Love. What a bold-faced lie! Reagan was elected governor of California. Lyndon B. Johnson increased troop presence in Vietnam, ignoring the massive demonstrations which rocked the nightly news. Several hundred thousand strong in New

York City alone. Race riots stormed through Cleveland, Detroit, Watts, Birmingham, Alabama, Rochester, New York, and dozens of other U.S. cities, inflaming tensions. Muhammad Ali was stripped of his World Heavyweight Championship for refusing the draft. Carl Wilson of the Beach Boys wouldn't go to war either and got tied up in a five-year legal battle which he eventually won. The Boston Strangler was sentenced to life in prison and escaped from the institution he was held in.

Bread was twenty-two cents a loaf, a gallon of gas was twenty-eight cents, and the inner-city ghetto which I called home was brimming with hard-working people with attitude and conviction whose lust for life couldn't be beaten out of them by piss-poor housing conditions, lousy pay, the police, or politicians. They taught me to fight for what I believed in, take pride in what I did, never give up, keep the faith, and, when hoping for a better tomorrow isn't enough, turn up the goddamn music and dance the blues away.

Well, you can take the wigger out of the ghetto, but you can't take the ghetto out of the wigger. After all, "The World Is a Ghetto." And even though I'll never forget my roots, I refused to allow them to strangle me by the ankles because even if I had to "Beg, Borrow, and Steal," this "Lightning's Girl" was going to be sure she was "Making Every Minute Count." Just like the radio taught me.

1967 helped to define who I was to become. I may have been too young to fully grasp the political implications of the time, but it started a fire in my belly that burns as bright today as it ever did. The National Organization for Women was officially incorporated in '67.

Grace Slick and Janis Joplin both threw down at the Monterey Pop Festival. Shirley Temple ran for Congress. I was just a tiny terror screaming my bloody head off to "Funky Broadway," already plotting my big city escape.

CANASTA

I can admit all of this now, only because I've lost everything I ever had. Including my soul. I feel little pieces of it breaking off and dissolving into dust like brittle petals on a ruined flower.

I was just a kid. A fucked-up little girl. Forced to grow up too quick. Too hard. Abandoned like a stowaway, shipwrecked into a life I never wanted to live. A life that felt like it was living me.

I felt like a mere spectator of inherited calamity whose origins trip back multiple generations, impregnating the very fabric of that ill-defined and terminally chronic condition called "family," where as an only child of an only child, I was forced to withstand all the abuse, tyranny, and trauma that is usually distributed equally amongst the brood.

There was only one direction the bat swung in, at my knees, causing them to buckle, collapse, corrode, crumple, felling me whenever, if even for a momentary interlude I felt I had finally landed on solid ground.

My mother split when I was thirteen. She tried and failed to raise me as friend, sidekick, mascot. You know how that works. I was made to play lure for sick and twisted old men, whose greasy eyes and wandering hands were an obvious threat to my future mental health.

But I guess I blew her trip. I couldn't play nice. Pissed her off. She felt threatened by my youth. It brought out the jealous, vindictive cunt that lurks beneath the temporal lobe of most alcoholic, middle-aged, and fading fast ex–beauty queen strippers turned switchboard operators down at the Last Ditch Motel.

My mother adored me when we were alone, when she was between johns, when she was lonely, desperate for attention, affection. She'd lavish me with sickly kisses and silly toys, stupid keepsakes, cheap key rings, charm bracelets, dumb trinkets. Mementos to her own fading luster once she could no longer stand to play witness to the funhouse mirror's twisted reflections as they ricocheted into an infinity of self-doubt and psychic lacerations, a homicidal force-field rifled with fear and loathing whose very nature attempted the murder of angels. And even though I was no angel, I was not yet the monster I was sure to become.

She dumped me with a father I had never met in a city I had never been to on the hottest day of the year, July 14, 1973. Retribution against my preemptive attack on her new boyfriend, "Uncle Randy."

One night, "Mom," which she despised being called, was out picking up some crappy Chinese take-away and a dime bag of pot, when even before she hit the corner store, her latest loser, an Appalachian ex-con with a rap sheet as long as his right arm, had already started in on me, cracking jokes about "Teenage pussy tastes like chicken chow mein and kumquats" and "Why don't you come over and keep my lap warm until your mother gets back," licking his chapped and cracked lips like a desert lizard flicking fly paper off his tongue.

He was tugging me toward him with a python grip around the nape of my neck, when in a fit of adolescent rage, fear, and repulsion fueled by the obnoxious proximity of his Pabst Blue Ribbon breath, I picked up a beer bottle and cracked him over the head, sending him reeling backward into the cheap plasterboard "entertainment center" which collapsed under his considerable weight, causing the stolen TV and dozens of eight-track tapes to clunk down upon his pea-brained nugget, spewing forth an acid rain of cigarette ash and bong water all over his dirty white wife beater which strained to contain his bowling ball–shaped blubber belly. I barreled out into the street screaming and laughing like a lunatic, running straight into my mother's arms, who took one look at me and screamed, "I can't trust you alone for five minutes!" as she ran into the house leaking a thin spittle of chow mein and egg drop soup up the sidewalk.

Heat wave hit Wayne County like a blister on a burn. And "Say hello to your daddy for me" was all she said the next afternoon as she banged on the fucked-up Impala's horn and threw me out the passenger door after luring me in for what I thought was going to be a picnic at Lake Wobegone, 120 miles south of the state line.

Last I saw of her.

My father was another story. He was never out of earshot. I was always at his side. Couldn't leave his sight. I became crutch, clutch, concubine. Maid, muse, wet nurse. Baby. Mommy. Girlfriend. Life support and ultimately death harbinger. Daddy knows best. How hateful little girls can be.

I never called him "Daddy," but it's still a word forever warped by everything he wasn't, a word that still rankles. Five letters and two simple syllables that instantly produce a nauseating metallic swell of the tongue, a blistering of the lips, a scraping razor burn akin to an esophageal Pap smear. A violent urge to regurgitate.

My father, that decrepit septic tank of treachery, that filter of perversity and lechery, a psychotic buffoon whose insidiously sadistic rituals polluted forever his every cancer-soaked brain cell, staining his fingers, toes, and tongue with a golden nicotine glow which seemed to swell and grow with every unfiltered cigarette he sucked down in an endless surrender to his own death, and to his daily massacre of whatever elegant morsel of humanity was left over inside me after the repeated soul rape of my mother's revolving-bedroom-door amours.

The weekend ritual. My father's specialty. A typical Friday night free-for-all where whatever was left of his pickled brains was further pummeled by booze into the brick wall of his own obliteration. Him and his asshole buddies. A permanent bender. Three out of seven days. For years on end. The memory still lingers.

One night during a marathon Black Jack match, I called Freddie Matolla "a fat-fuck huckster" and told him to keep his filthy hands to himself. The bloated chimp had one hand up my short plaid skirt and a blistered thumb hitched under my panty line ready to yank them aside.

My asshole father butted in under his breath with the threat that if I wanted a place to sleep that night, I show some respect, play sweetmeat, swallow it down, and let it slide. No harm in a little snuggle. Go on and give Uncle Freddie a smooch. No one had to tell me that what starts with a kiss usually ends with a fisting.

I told them both to fuck off and got my right ear boxed with a rubber plunger. It rang like Sunday school church bells for two days after. But I was always getting cracked in the head. Enough times to occasionally crumple into contusion, usually for saying something I wasn't supposed to, or NOT doing something I was supposed to, or for skulking the South Side Slopes, prowling the streets for a wandering eyeball or two, a stray gaze, that thousand-mile stare set somewhere behind the black and baby blues of the sunken skulls of lonely low-life losers. Wasted pasty mama's boys who I'd sucker up to and into my sex, baiting them in with fraudulent promises of pussy ever after. If they could just buck up, grind down, and do the time for my petty crimes.

Looking for more of that negative attention—the only kind I ever got at home. The only kind I'll ever be able to truly respond to. The kind I blame my mother for forcing me to suffer after she ran off with some two-bit snitch—couldn't stand the sight of her little bitch ruining all the fun . . .

But then I'm jumping the gun here, rallying prematurely, and all this ballyhooing is the result of what I'm about to detail, not the reason it all happened in the first place. Little that I did endeared me to Pops, who not only despised my mother and their short-lived Jersey Shore summer affair, but used me as target for retribution against the responsibility he had always rebuked.

He tolerated me only now, after more than a decade of dismissing my existence, because just on the cusp of puberty, my body scented with the bloom of youth, my beauty about to blossom, my boobs about to bust forth, I was the "big-draw money raker" at his Hanover Haven Strong-Arm Street Sweeps, his weekly Canasta game. Four rowdy louts dumbly clustered around him with fists full of singles they were dead set on losing, encouraging his raging assholism which they applauded and supplemented with a stupidity that was somehow touchingly disgusting, and horrendously moronic.

A real armchair philosopher complete with his own fat and fucked-up fan club, Pop's line of reasoning was, "Do as I say, not as I do" . . . "Shoot first, ask questions later," and, "You can't win for losing" . . . although I gotta hand it to the ass-wipe, if you could've, he would've . . . ten times over.

Two months into my residency, when my dad, the dick, who would have gambled on a cockroach race if they had a window for it down at the local OTB, was hosting another Friday-night blow-out and losing big time. By now down 732 bucks . . . wanting to even the score and having nothing left to barter since his car had been impounded by Dick Chase's auto body shop for the better part of that year due to lack of payment, he decided to put ME up on the auction block. That filthy skunk. He had already forfeited the lawn mower, his power tools, the living room couch, and his shaving kit. The stakes suddenly tripled. Allow me to break it down . . .

The five shits sat in a circle. A round table littered with half a dozen overflowing coffee cans filled with the diseased butts of two hundred Chesterfields, Pall Malls, Viceroys, Camels, and two or three still spit-soaked White Owls whose gummed-to-death tips acted as magnet to cellophane, ash, and fingernail clippings. The browning air was moist and heavy with the mordant aroma that only men on the brink of drinking and smoking themselves into that big unfit sleep are steeped in.

The sticky floor had been pissed on by the slippery-dick trickle of Schlitz, Coors, Jim Beam, Jack Daniel's, and Johnnie Walker Red. The carcasses of thousands of split peanut shells sang a stupid song to the broken bones that had been prevented at least for tonight, by the five lechers who were gathered around the bare, moth-specked forty-watt bulb at my father's precariously perched three-legged dining room table.

By 9:15 they were all shit-faced. Drunk as fuck and squealing like the insufferable sex pigs that they were. I was forced to play waitress, barkeep, and Barbie doll. Keep their busted cups full of rotgut, the pickled pigs feet coming, the corn dogs warm, and smile like I meant it. Yeah, right . . . Give me something to smile about, assholes.

I don't think I even learned to crack a grin until I was fourteen, and then only used it as a rouse to lure lousy dirt boys into bed with me in the hopes of pilfering their wallets. But that came later.

The aforementioned Fat Freddie Matolla, who sold little old ladies burial plots for their future grandchildren, was hijacking the ante up, trying to force the other monkeys to throw down their cards, slapping happy at his porky thighs, hoping to score a big wet one while chewing on my virgin tenderloin.

Jersey Joe di Blasco, small-time hood and part-time security guard down at the local bingo hall, was sweating blood. Tongue wagging like a side of beef swinging. The ring around his collar leaving dirt stains on his greasy neck. Mighty Mike Junco was contemplating a winning streak. Defined by his cauliflower ears as ex-amateur wrestler with a federation so small it had only two initials, he was punching the air with a Brooklyn cheer, sitting not so pretty on a pair of tens, grinning like a lunatic. I feared he'd pop a hole in his shit-sluiced shorts, exposing his hard-on which was straining the worn brown corduroy of his high-waters.

Deano la Martino, a sleazy sad-sack Italian door-to-door vacuum cleaner salesman, with a pencil-thin salt-and-pepper mustache used as peanut shell crumb catcher, henpecked to near death by a high-maintenance beauty salon addict and her four intolerable bastard kids, was the only half-humanoid left who could still wager a bet. He looked so morose I thought he had burst his colos-tomy bag. He struggled with the winning hand know-ing full well in order to save face, and in the meantime maybe my ass, at least from the other baby killers, that he'd have to go through with it. He'd have to claim his booty. *Me.* And off we went to my father's bedroom.

I have to hand it to the motherfucker: For a loopy old shit, my dad had it made. He spent most of his waking hours in bed, nursing his "disability," a bum knee he was still collecting on from a construction accident a decade earlier. He'd be propped up against the natty, floral print–covered, four-poster king-sized bed, stoned on Vicodin, Darvon, and Percocet, jerking off to after-noon soaps, ringing a fucking dinner bell for service, ordering up a triple-decker grilled bologna-and-cheese sandwich smothered in ketchup and a six-pack. When feeling swank he'd demand two Swanson Hungry-Man turkey TV dinners with a back of Jack like he was king rhino at Blue Beard's Brothel.

Red-velvet Victorian wallpaper, floor to ceiling, framed a mastadonian-sized dresser with cracked mirror to match. The only women who ever stepped foot inside this loser's lair left fifty dollars richer. He'd cut their pictures out of the trashy weekly trade papers, get them to autograph them with candy-colored lipstick kisses, and then brag about it later. It even smelled of porno. That cheap fucking pig. Bartering my cherry off for a lousy card game. I could have killed him. It was rumored that I eventually did.

But back to Deano. He was as sloppy and sloshed as the other four shitbags who were part and parcel of this hideous charade, banging the table with their empty beer bottles, pounding out a weird tattoo. Chanting and caterwauling like a pack of sick circus clowns at a small-town weekend rodeo.

Deano takes me by the hand, making a dainty little show of kissing me on top of my head, waltzing me around the table, yanking on my striped tank top, revealing my snow-white training bra. Whoops and hollers follow. Jersey Joe grabs a hank of hair and slobbers on my neck. Mighty Mike pinches my left cheek and twists. Fat Freddie grabs once again for my ass. My dad laughs like he's showing off a prize-winning porker at a pig farm. I cringe, shrink, and forget where I am. I experience my first blackout.

I come to flat on my back in my father's bed. The smell of vinegar, whiskey, and shit gagging me back to life. The pricks must've carried me in. Deano's trying to get his dick hard, but Jim Beam won't let him.

He's as soft as a little girl. Tears are streaming down his face. "Jesus, Mary, and Joseph, have mercy . . ." he trails off. He's so pathetic I burst out laughing. But laughing makes him angry. When he's angry he gets hard. When he's hard he's got to use it.

Deano, it seems, through tear-stained confessions, doesn't stay hard for too long. It's the reason his wife's having an affair . . . He can no longer get it up . . . his kids hate him . . . they make fun of him . . . call him *Silly Putty*, after hearing his wife complain one too many times through plasterboard walls about what a lousy lay he is . . . "Jesus, even the kids know . . ." he moans.

All revealed between nasty pulls on his now hard, now limp "thing." He begs me to take it in my mouth. To kiss it . . . just a little . . . to mouth a prayer to the Virgin of Guadalupe on its ugly purple tip . . . "You're still a virgin, right? Maybe you'll cure me . . . Please just try . . . just this once." His heartbreak is obvious. I'm overcome with pity. Self-disgust. I put the shrunken head in my mouth. It tastes like a soft pretzel soaked in saltwater. He pats me gently on the head. Praying again to Mary. The soft dough starts to rise. Swells, bubbles up, gets sticky.

Deano panics. Plops it out of my mouth. Pushes me back on the bed. Shoves the bread stick inside me. The first time he thrusts, it hurts. Him. "Easy! Easy! Easy!" he wails at me. I giggle, amazed. He immediately goes soft again. Swirls it around outside until it garners a bit of heft. He tries to force it back in. It's semi-soft. But the buttery roll folds in upon itself. In desperation, he jacks it up and down so hard, he gets a Charlie horse in both legs, causing him to flap and flail around on the bed braying like an electric donkey or spastic piñata being pummeled by hundreds of invisible blows, until screaming, he squirts one or two drops of gooey gluey paste, which land on my right shoe as he rolls over and buries his head in his hands crying, "Oh, dear God, Immaculate Mary, Sweet Baby Jesus, what have I just done . . . ?"

There is safety and comfort in this ritualized disintegration. A sense of homo-pathetic male bonding. On Monday morning, when these five sacks of living puss and puke wake up, they will not remember their diseased lust. They will have erased all traces of their own malignant guilt and once more embraced the lies they have based their subhuman existence on. They will, after their first blurry-eyed beer of the day, congratulate themselves. Proud to have formulated a ridiculous credo based on the outlandish belief that by working 9 to 5 five days a week at shitty, low-paying, brain-dead, minimum-wage slave labor camps, the respect and human dignity that they have been so rightfully denied their entire lives has now been earned in transmutation by their brutarian mistreatment of me, who in a cruel reversal of fate, is made to feel as filthy and degenerate as they truly are.

PART II

CUNTZILLA

ELUSIVE BITCH

I love Sleep, that elusive bitch, but Sleep hates me. Just the way it is. I can't seduce her into tolerating me for more than a few hours a night. Fickle cunt. Oh, she'll allow me into her warm embrace. Five minutes after my head hits the pillows, I'll be swimming into a delicious nocturnal numbness. But before REM has a chance to cock his nugget against mine, Sleep, that fricking creep, screams for her night nurse Insomnia to kick me in the head like a bouncer at a funeral party, and faster than you can say *the quick and the dead*, I no longer am. Asleep that is. Bitch.

I've tried over-the-counter as well as various prescribed medications, including, but not limited to Klonopin, Ativan, Halcion, Xanax, Valium, melatonin, marijuana, valerian root, and heroin. I've tortured myself with exhaustive workouts followed by hot baths preceding tantric sex where I practiced deep breathing in conjunction with meditation and visualization techniques.

I gave up nicotine, sugar, spice, and tried a light box. Didn't help. I quit coffee. HA! Anyone who has suffered from decades-long Insomnia knows damn well that that ain't gunna last. You need all the caffeine you can suck down to function above that semi-somnambulant state of dream-deprived Sleep that results in a numb narcosis, a permanent twilight zone, rarely fully conscious, never completely asleep. Exhausted, but jacked up, like an electric rigor mortis that short circuits the neurotransmitters creating a dense fog of chronic irritation that can cloud even the simplest of tasks.

I am not referring to a few nights or even months of unfit Sleep. Nor the youthful buzz which invigorates the blood stream, rife with recollections of uncountable naughty deeds performed under the influence of designer cocktails. No, this miserable ditty is a song of the sirens to the janitors of lunacy who have certainly not made peace, for there is none to be made, after nearly half a century of stalking Morpheus, that cruel trickster who only grants the occasional performance, and then upon a stage so soaked with blood and guts that the sheer magnitude of his insane cruelty creates a magnificent terror from which one is throttled awake, soaked in sweat, choked by tears and stifling a scream, which unleashed would wake the very dead themselves, those lucky bastards to whom Sleep is an eternal given.

Even in the cradle, I couldn't sleep. I can recollect conversations I was too young to fully decipher. The winning hand held by my father on a typical Friday-night poker marathon. The date the gas bill was due. Useless drivel. I started Sleepwalking at six. Talking to the electric sockets in the living room. Directing traffic in my pajamas. Urinating in the refrigerator. Suffocating my younger brother with a ratty teddy bear. By the age of nine, already terminally Sleep deprived, my nightmares were so gruesome that horror films read like bad comedies to my twisted preadolescent psyche.

Youth feeds on adrenaline. Who needs sleep when you're a rambunctious teenager carousing through the night gallery of new experience? Or a rampaging twenty-something hell-bent on accomplishing as much as possible, living life to the fullest, glutting on potential, and wilding in the streets desperate to make your mark before that grump Thanatos comes calling. And what the hell . . . I'LL SLEEP WHEN I'M DEAD becomes the young psycho's mantra screamed into the crack of an unforgiving Dawn who is always able to creep up on you faster than you could ever dream of outrunning her.

For most of my life I just didn't need more than four hours of Sleep a night. I felt great, I glowed, got a shitload of work done, Loved the twilight hours between 3 and 6 a.m. when the rest of the world died or at least wasn't crawling up my ass with its noise, its complaints, its problems and demands. But enough is enough; or let me rephrase that: Now there just isn't enough. Ever.

I am jolted awake after a three-hour stint kissing Slumber. Cheap bastard kicks me out of bed and snickers as I begin my night watch. He will not welcome me back into his cozy surround for at least another twenty hours. Doesn't matter how exhausted, drained, or in pain I am. And pain happens. Migraines multiply when you are running on fumes. A throbbing band of tension expands outward from the temples threatening to shatter the skull. The bones in your face splinter into glass shards exiting through your eye sockets. Vision blurs. Breathing becomes shallow. Your shoulders spasm and lock, grinding into your neck, freezing ligaments. Chronic Sleep deprivation encourages the build-up of toxins in the body, creating a permanent irritability. You're always itchy somewhere under the skin, between the muscle and bone, deep inside the tissue. Tendons are scraped raw as if infected by an army of slow-moving insects whose miniscule mandibles rub together in delight as every inch of skin stings. The eyes twitch. The temples throb. The brain bleeds.

But, after all, what's one more day, month, decade robbed of Sleep and stuck squirming in a state of agitated limbo-essence, when you have an eternity of peace to eventually look forward to? That is, if you are foolish enough to believe that yes, death will be peaceful. It will caress like black velvet those shattered nerves and twisted muscles that have revolted now for so long that even beyond the grave they may still be screaming for relief. A relief like deep Sleep, which I am convinced I may never, not in this lifetime or the next, ever experience.

MOTHERHOOD:
IT'S NOT COMPULSORY

He's nineteen months old pushing a fire engine-red go-cart across the driveway. Perfectly formed almond eyes bespeak the mystery and intrigue his limited vocabulary will never mouth. Our eyes lock upon each other. Instant hypnosis. His motor functions freeze. He drops his toy and barrels at me as fast as his little feet will fly. Grips my thighs. Attempts to crawl up my body, and with a little boost my two hands cradle him under his arms, raise him to my face, and kiss his nose. He wraps his pudgy baby legs around my hips, pets my hair, burrows his head in my neck, and coos. All is motherly bliss, until he shits his diaper. The smell rises. My clothes reek. His real mommy is headed our way. She wants him back. Thank God. She can have him. At least until he's twelve.

I love children and they love me. Years of plane, train, and bus travel have helped me to master the secret of forging an unspoken allegiance with kids of all ages. On interminable ten-hour transatlantic journeys, for the sake of not only myself but the rest of my fellow travelers, if I hear a child crying I will immediately seek out the source of the yowling little nipper, and take matters into my own hands. I can assure you peace will quickly be restored. The once ferocious battle cry whose very resonance threatened to break the sound barrier is instantaneously replaced with a soft chuckling, a tender purr, a benign smile. Baby Love.

It could be my circus-red hair, the pheromones I excrete, or the look of pity, empathy, and total understanding that emanates from my very own baby blues, but infants, (not to mention dogs and men alike) have an uncanny urge to please Big Momma and usually do so by dropping down to all fours, crawling around at my feet, quickly quieting down, and burying their runny little snouts under my armpits, between my legs, or in my breast. Often accompanied by a soul-shuddering sigh so completely neutralizing it borders on a mild neurological orgasm. Of course, I need a lithium douche to feel half human again after my own chemical makeup has been momentarily skewered by the lingering afterglow of baby drool sponged off my shirt collar. Now isn't that cute???

My maternal instincts kick in to spite me. I hate to hear babies cry. Hell, I hate to hear anyone cry. It's the most obnoxious form of noise pollution. And if all it takes to temporarily abate this skin-crawling caterwaul is a quick snatch which lifts the little bantamweight crying time bomb into my arms to give it a tight squeeze and a peck on the cheek, who am I to argue? After all, "Mother" knows best . . . which both amazes and horrifies the real birth mom. Who may indeed enjoy the respite, yet whose first instinct is to grab the little critter and flee as far away as humanly possible so as to rescue her precious little angel from the unforeseen and imaginary evil of an obviously over-sexed baby freak.

However, upon hearing the opening stanza of the Terror of Tiny Town's latest lung-busting operetta, Mommy usually gives in, Baby wins out, and I'm stuck playing bouncy-wouncy with the twenty-pound flesh ball for the next eight hours. Not a problem. I understand children. It's their mothers I can't fucking stand.

Every new mother believes her little cherub is the most awe-inspiring angel to ever be shat forth upon this ungodly planet. The endlessly exaggerated delight over the little darlings first coo, goo, drool, burp, barf, and poop becomes a tireless tirade whose glorification of the most foul bodily functions insults not only the intelligence, but the patience of every ear within a ten-mile Toys"R"Us radius. A nonstop daily update tumbles forth in fits and starts from the lips of the first-time mother's mundanity-strewn mouth, as if the size, smell, and consistency of the little shitter's latest bowel movement is in itself news, and not merely the sandwich meat of sea gull roughage down at your local landfill, where disposable diapers by the tens of millions, which have a half-life of about ten thousand years, in a flagrant disregard to future generations, will forever swelter and billow in noxious sky-blue and pink clouds, further contaminating an already toxic landscape whose single most environmentally hazardous threat to the planet is the SIX BILLION other greedy babies who live to eat, shit, piss, consume, and make waste enough to result in a non-biodegradable garbage barge piled sky high from here to the moon and back again. And I thought the smell of one of the little poopy troopers was befouling enough to behold. Hold your breath and smile. The average four-year-old has already soiled more than 2,595 Pampers before he or she hits kindergarten. And then the real fun, bed wetting, kicks in. At least bed sheets are recyclable.

I shot out my biological time clock before it even punched itself in. The mortifying thought of actually having an alien life form develop inside my body terrifies me. I can barely stand to live inside my own flesh. Call me inhuman, but childbirth gives me the creeps. It seems the single most unnatural act that a woman would ever consciously perpetrate against herself. As if the ritual abuse of sex isn't grotesque enough, a nine-month gestation period follows, which begins after a single sperm cell worms its slimy way in and infects a fertile egg, resulting in the glorious wonder that is morning sickness, vomiting, insatiable craving for junk food, sore back, ballooning breasts, weight gain, and funny-looking clothes that don't fit. This honeymoon from Hell is capped off with the eventual expulsion of a nine-pound sack of blood and mucous with the vocal range of a shrieking demon who will for the next three years be forever demanding tit, diaper changing, and constant affection. I can't even afford to pay that much non-stop attention to myself. It would make me sick, I'd turn homicidal and go fucking postal in about three days.

Let's not even begin to discuss the horror of the possibility of an eighteen-hour-long delivery, where shitting out a watermelon would by comparison be a cakewalk in the park. My theory is if it doesn't fit *in*, it won't come *out*. And until you've seen a live broadcast of a C-Section you have no idea just how medieval modern medicine really is. After the evil smiley-face incision is carved in the lower abdomen, the mad doctor removes your uterus, as in *lifting it out of your body*, brushing aside the blood and guts with a Betadine hose down, painting an even more gory picture of the real meaning of the Hippocratic oath, as he forces the little devil out of its morbid hiding place, restitching the permanent damage already done as casually as darning an old sock with size-ten knitting needles. Heinous. Horrible. Count me out.

Besides, the truth of the matter is, all the men I know are still fucking babies. They all demand to be coddled, handled with kid gloves, spoon-fed, sent to obedience school, and even on the odd occasion, spanked in a way that only a *real mother* would truly know how. These services I am more than happy to oblige. It's always at most a part-time job, not a lifelong commitment. Or, as the New York Board of Education once so astutely promoted in an subway ad campaign against teenage motherhood: *It's like being grounded for eighteen years!*

And at least I know that none of them will grow up to one day hate my goddamn guts because try as I may, I just couldn't supply the parasitic lechers with everything their greedy little hearts desired. Men may be babies, but unlike the little leeches, they thrive on neglect, abuse, and abandonment. They may cry and stamp their feet in order to suckle on Mother's Milk, but they won't starve to death if they don't get it. One word of advice: Next time "the urge" to procreate kicks in, close your legs, shut your mouth, grab the closest man, stick his rash-covered ass in an adult-sized Depends diaper, hold him in your arms, and feed him your left tit for forty-five minutes every three hours for the next week. I hope it forces you to reconsider exactly what the "joy of motherhood" is really all about.

ASSUME THE POSITION

Blame it on Bobby Blake. I was still wearing knee socks and selling Girl Scout cookies when *Baretta* hit the air. He reminded me of my father. Or how I wanted my father to be. Only Dad and Baretta were on opposite sides of the law. Baretta went after bad guys. My dad *was* a bad guy. But Baretta didn't save me. And in an attempt to reverse the outcome, I've been looking for someone who can "protect and serve" ever since. Not to keep me safe, but to penalize for their inability to do so.

My first face-to-face with the police jump-started a decades-long obsession with testing just how far I could twist the long arm of the law to satisfy my criminal intent. I was babysitting for fifty cents an hour. Chump change needed to keep an already overheated and horny thirteen-year-old stoned on lousy Mexican weed. I had just finished blowing a skinny joint. Went outside to check on the ghetto rats I was supposed to play Mommy to. Found them rolling around on the ground, one of them screaming, "If that's all you got, keep it in your shorts, shithead," as a dirty chartreuse Pontiac sped left around the corner. The freak behind the wheel had snaked alongside the back fence, which bordered the alley, and beckoned the girls over to ask for directions; Cindy said he had a funny look in his eye. "Maybe it was because he was squirting dick juice all over the steering wheel," Kathy, the younger one, screeched, jerking on the handle of her dirty jump rope. I admired her potential as mouthpiece for future S.C.U.M. *Manifesto* fundraisers; but this was serious. They were obviously too young to fully comprehend the offensive maneuvers of a drive-by jack-off artist. I had no choice. They were in my care. I called the cops.

Officer Connolly was a twenty-one-year-old rookie. Blond, blue-eyed, built. Been on the force only six months. We hit the backyard to investigate the crime scene. Tire tracks and a spent Chesterfield. He pocketed the butt. Pulled out pen and pad, chicken-scratching notes. Looking real official. Claimed he'd investigate. I plopped down on a lawn chair across from him, making sure to spread my legs just wide enough for him to notice the crotch of my tight jeans disappearing. *Investigate this Office, sir.* I can assure you, I was not suffering from arrested development.

My baby blues were glued to his equipment. Nightstick, handcuffs, revolver. Hot. I couldn't help it. Had to milk it. I confessed I was withholding evidence. I had failed to report that a similar make car had pulled the same stunt on me three weeks before. Obviously a perv was lurking. I was sure I'd recognize the creep. He suggested cruising the neighborhood to search for the perpetrator once my babysitting shift was done. Looking nervously over his shoulder, he adjusted his gun holster.

"Are you flirting with me Officer Connolly?" I demurred.

"Typical police procedure," he assured me. HA!

I hate to play snitch, but I penned my own version of "Fuck tha Police" four hours later. The back of the squad car stunk of vomit, urine, and Old Spice. I was frisked, read my rights, interrogated, and strip-searched. But only after threatening to report the rookie to the station chief if he wouldn't play Bad Lieutenant. My career in blackmailing, public indecency, criminal misconduct, disturbing the peace, and assaulting an officer of the law just for kicks had just begun.

I've never had a beef with the police. Never been hassled, harassed, or assaulted by the cops. They, however, can't say the same thing about me. Poor saps. I was arrested only once. Helsinki, Finland, 1982. The shifty musician I was traveling with was busted for smuggling illegal substances into the country. I was innocent, but taken into custody. The twin Tom of Finland customs officers guarding my cell allowed me to keep my bag. Big mistake. I slipped into a peach satin slip, pulled out a pint of Smirnoff Red, nibbled on a piece of Godiva chocolate, and began seducing both of them by reading chapters of Jerzy Kosinski's *Cockpit*. Needless to say, the charges were dropped.

I love cops and the cops love me. Got the evidence to prove it. I've shot dozens of photographs of police officers. Just ask literary outlaw Jerry Stahl.

March 2003 we rampaged through Florida, terrorizing the locals. Hit-and-run spoken word spree. We hijacked a 747 to Orlando, made a public nuisance of ourselves, verbally battered the audience, ripped off the promoter, committed grievous bodily harm to a couple of unwitting victims, and split town before bothering to clean the blood off our hands. We knocked off a rental joint and started tooling north in an air-conditioned 2003 Neon. A perfectly anonymous getaway car.

Giddy as a pair of short-shift grifters on the run from L.A., cranking tunes and laughing like lunatics, the first heist went off without a hitch. We owned the fucking road, man. Until the short stabs of a police siren sounded, we got blasted in the back of the head with red lights, and were instructed to pull over just outside of St. Pete. The bull sauntered over to the driver's seat, smiling. "Is there a problem, officer?" quipped Stahl, deadpan. Deputy Sheriff R. Sammons assured us we weren't speeding and that he was just checking us out because we "looked too cool for Alligator Alley." I invited him to the show later that night. Told him we played tag team to the themes of power and submission, crime and punishment, retribution and restitution. Publicly confessed our own crimes and punished the audience by making them pay to hear the grisly details. He chuckled but politely declined. Duty called.

Jerry knew what was coming next. I'd be forced to shoot. I'd already been showing off a stash of photos from our last tour. Cops on bikes, cops drinking coffee at a pastry stand, geriatric cops, and Jerry's favorite, a *Baywatch*-blond law-enforcement agent in tight blue spandex shorts bending over the front seat of her squad car to retrieve her business card so I could send her duplicate prints.

I waited until Sammons was behind the wheel. I jumped out of the Neon. Flagged him over. Used my trademark, "Excuse me, sir, I'm doing a series entitled *People Who Help People*. Would you mind if I take a shot or two?" Faking an innocent smile, I'd point to my camera, stare them straight in the eye, and hypnotize them with a sociopathic ability to divorce the guilty party from the crimes committed. Not a single cop has ever refused me.

I've got mug shots, telephone numbers, job offers, and propositions for dates, drinks, and drive-alongs. I've had police escorts through long lines at the airport. I once bribed a Russian cop with a French kiss to steal another officer's cap, convincing him I'd only impersonate a cop in the privacy of my own home. In public I'm usually found screaming bloody murder and implicating myself in crimes too numerous to mention to ever cast doubt upon this career criminal's twisted convictions.

The benchmark of a good crime is to avoid getting caught. Keep it under the radar. I've successfully avoided detection, prosecution, and imprisonment while continuing to perpetrate my felonious behavior. So I couldn't help but question whether or not the e-mail that arrives in June of 2003 is a set-up, a fraud, or an invitation to commit the ultimate con. I roll the dice and decide to up the ante. Two high-stakes gamblers sporting backgrounds in art crimes sucker me into their latest scam. Play infiltrator and interrogator for *Where Are They When We Don't Need Them?* a documentary they're filming on the tenth World Police and Fire Games. A biannual sports event held that year in Barcelona, Spain, which like the rest of Europe is suffering under the worst heat wave in 200 years.

Over the course of two weeks, 10,000 law-enforcement agents and firefighters compete for gold, silver, and bronze medals in sixty different sporting events. Wrestling, weight lifting, soccer, archery, darts, tug-of-war, pistol combat, bowling. Think Olympics. Only with crime stoppers and firefighters.

The World Police and Fire Games originated in Los Angeles in 1985, in part to boost flagging police morale, encourage camaraderie among cops and firefighters, and to improve public relations between the police and civilians. I can't imagine a more intoxicating way to spend my summer vacation.

I arrive at LAX at 2:40 p.m., what I believe to be a safe two hours in advance of British Airways flight 422. So sick of traveling I'm nearly comatose with boredom. The traffic en route to the airport. The failure of electronic check-in. The gaudy spectacle of out-of-shape American families dressed in matching pastel tracksuits. And now the latest insult. British Airways has instituted a new and highly invasive procedure. Passengers form a long line before reaching the check-in desk. Bags are screened first, then an overage bag boy personally escorts you to the next long line. Usually I wouldn't have a problem with this. But how to explain the small red bag inside the larger black bag, which contains fifty feet of black quarter-inch rope, pliers, nipple, clamps, two wigs, and six corsets? Don't ask. Fortunately, sex toys have not yet been ruled a terrorist threat and I slide by without being strip-searched.

I land a mind-numbing fifteen hours later. Exhausted, sleep deprived, hot, and starving. But duty calls. My partner in crime meets me at the airport, offers me a Coke, sticks a pill in my mouth, and instructs me to swallow. Time to face the firing squad. Or at least pick up my press pass. Arriving just in time for the last few events means we'll have to work fast.

Nearly every cop I've ever talked to, when asked why he opted to go into law enforcement, responds, "To help people." Can you imagine actually calling the cops if you ever really needed help in Los Angeles? What if Officer Jeremy Morse, Mark Fuhrman, or Rafael "Rampart Scandal" Pérez answered the call?

Were these testosterone-fueled Dirty Harrys just freaks with short fuses or indicative of the corruption and abuse of power within law-enforcement agencies the world over? Was a competitive sporting event really a good idea for macho men whose motto was supposed to be *To Protect and Serve*? Whose presence more often than not inspires fear and dread?

According to the officers I spoke with in Barcelona, an event like WPFG has a positive effect on the individual, who through the discipline of their chosen sport is able to return to the field with more stamina and patience because they have found a place to focus their aggressions.

Cops and firefighters from Siberia, Korea, Thailand, Denmark, Poland, China, South Africa, North America, Canada, and just about every other country on the map, had paid their own way to honor the homeland. Hunky, hard-working men as far as the eye can see, sweating, grunting, fighting, shooting, all pumped up to just be there, participating in these events like thousands of well-lubed gladiators. Win or lose, they'd already proven they were tough enough to make the grade. They were there to throw down, have a good time, hang out with the brotherhood, and represent. I couldn't think of a more deliciously perverse event to have been in the thick of.

The video crew and I hit the billiards competition, tae kwon do, tug-of-war, pistol shooting, and weight lifting events all in one day. What bliss! Surrounded by modern-day warriors, slapping each other on the ass, kissing and hugging, cracking jokes, and more than happy to submit to my fanatical grilling concerning marijuana reform laws in Canada, mandatory minimum sentencing, the stress of being underpaid, overworked, and feared, the negative image of the Los Angeles Police Department, and, of course, how they were planning to celebrate at the closing ceremony. The Australian Beer Blast being the unanimous response.

Being jacked-up after witnessing so many high-impact sports, and wilting in the 102-degree swelter, although not high on my list of priorities, we head over to investigate the bowling alley. Expecting a gang of retired gentlemen quietly polishing their balls, I stumble in to a lager-and–Red Bull bash where howling madmen are congratulating each other by tossing back pints of the evil brew, insisting I join them in making merry.

"Pinkie," a pit bull of a man, at six-foot-two and a solid 270 pounds, is not to be denied. Sporting a *Simpson's* Springfield Police shirt whose insignia bears a patch of Chief Wiggum, he has just won a silver medal. Squashing me with a bone-crushing bear hug, he waltzes me around the bar introducing me to the British Metropolitan Police Service as the "next Ruby Wax."

His drunken glee is contagious. He throws me into the arms of gold medal winner in singles bowling, Officer John Greengrass. Who has a fetching scar running halfway from elbow to wrist. I ask if it's a bowling injury. He chuckles, winks, and struts, "In a manner of speaking, yes." Greengrass and a fellow officer were returning to London after the last WPFG held in Indianapolis. Heading home from Heathrow, a car chase breaks out. They get stuck between a stolen car and a speeding paddy wagon. Unable to just sit idly by, Greengrass instructs his pal, the driver, to "do something . . . we're police officers!" They pull over. The carjacker is careening toward them. Greengrass, fueled on by the smell of burning rubber and adrenaline, jumps from the car, grabbing his bowling bag which is loaded with two deadly eighteen-pounders. Raising the bag high overhead, he aims for the windshield, smashing it to slivers. The surprise attack stops the vehicle, but not before chewing a chunk out of his right forearm. They arrest the thief. I ask if he showed him "the what for." "Of course not," he smirked. "The kid was only thirteen." I volunteered that I would have spanked him myself given half a chance. "Best leave the punishment to the professionals," he chuckled, then winked and fingered his gold medal. I couldn't agree more.

Update: In March 2007 I received an e-mail from Officer John Greengrass, politely inquiring whether I remembered our meeting. HA! I never forget a cop I might have future use for. He requested a favor. Would I be so kind as to record a short video hello for the London Metropolitan Police, who were about to celebrate the fortieth anniversary of their bowling league? I couldn't resist. I ended my message with a wink, a slick grin, and a joke about bowlers and the size of their balls. Big'uns. Gotta love 'em.

"IN TIMES OF UNIVERSAL DECEIT, TELLING THE TRUTH IS A REVOLUTIONARY ACT" —GEORGE ORWELL

It took balls for Elton John to suggest banning all organized religion because it turned people into hateful lemmings devoid of compassion. And I may be putting my cock on the line here, but I think we need to go directly to the source and simply get rid of God. After all, God was the first cop. The original tyrant. An egotistical dictator whose sadism was so immense that he insisted on the murder of his only begotten son just to prove what he was capable of after he condemned us all to rot in eternal damnation like flesh puppets in his own private dungeon. An amusement arcade full of fire and brimstone.

Religion used to be the opium of the masses. Now it's the crack cocaine of assassins. Millions of addicts tripping on a celestial high. Throwing psychotic temper tantrums like little brats who forgot to take their Ritalin. Backyard bullies screaming, "MY GOD IS BIG-GER THAN YOUR GOD." God junkies—dangerous and delirious. Drunk on blood and bombs and the smell of burning flesh. Painting the desert red in an attempt to appease BIG POPPA, that vengeful Warlord whose favorite blood sport has always been one of violence, torture, and retribution.

War is as old as God himself. And the War is never over. The War is never ending. The War is just an orgy of blood and guts masterminded by testosterone-fueled dirty old men who get off on fucking the entire planet. This is the REAL PORNOGRAPHY. An outrageous cock-fight fought by gung-ho cowboys who have drawn a line in the sand and will challenge anyone to a duel foolish enough to threaten resistance against the advent of the rodeo mind.

Man was not created in the image of God. God was created in the image of man so that man had someone to blame his infantile rage on. The need to believe in God is a pathological viral infection which has spread like an incurable disease infecting man's ability to reason clearly. Belief acts as a psychic buffer against anxiety over the un-avoidable reality of impending mortality. Scared shitless and still greedy for more than merely earthly delights, man, that all-consuming piranha, has wreaked havoc by gobbling up and devouring every other creature, forcing predictions that unless a miracle happens even the fish will be wiped out before the middle of this century. It's no wonder then that man looks to the heavens for his next fix, dreaming of an endless bounty to be served up by angels and virgins alike, assuming it's the just dessert of a hard-fought battle, a Holy War waged against the evil of others. Against the infidels and devils.

War as we know it will never end. As long as we continue to allow religious fanatics, fundamentalists, madmen, and maniacs to carry on this millennium-old charade where battles are fought for the glory of

God and country, and the army with the most money wins.

Maybe War is just menstrual envy. Maybe if men bled every month as much as I do, they wouldn't have such incredible blood lust. Maybe I'm dreaming. I also realize that in the past I would have been burned at the stake, another heretic exterminated during the menstrual murders perpetrated by the witch hunts of the Middle Ages. A War which raged for 400 years instigated by the Church and its holy redeemers based upon a campaign of fear and loathing. Strikingly similar to the massacres still being propagated by self-righteous apocalypticians today.

Am I imagining it or were we a lot safer when the so-called leader of the free world was getting blowjobs in the White House? Isn't it better to blow off a little steam in the face of a willing victim than to take out your sexual frustrations and pent-up aggression on countries half-way around the world, blatantly lying about democracy and freedom in a thinly veiled disguise to suck the juice out of a hole in the ground, while the rest of us are stuck at the Exxon stations holding gas pumps in our fists like big limp dicks that we pay out the ass to get perpetually screwed by?

We inhabit a vast potential Utopia which is being destroyed by its abusers. Man has created a Hell on earth, turning the world into a ghetto, a slaughterhouse, a refugee camp, an orphanage, a sweatshop, a bomb factory, a land mine, a shooting gallery, an insane asylum, a toxic dump. And the way I see it, Mother Nature is getting pretty pissed off. Earthquakes, tornadoes, floods, mudslides, hurricanes, droughts, monsoons, famine.

She is becoming more violent against the men who cause her violence.

And maybe, after all, violence is only natural. All Creation bears the molecular memory of a terrible explosion of electricity, energy, matter, and motion. A violent eruption of white light and white heat. Violence was the first act of creation. THE BIG BANG. Chaos is the law of Nature, it is the score upon which reality is written. The Universe is just geometry stricken with epilepsy. Creation, a nightmare spectacle. Life, a trembling accident. We are all just germinating here on this hothouse planet which has been soaked with the blood of all its creatures for hundreds of thousand of years now. Or to quote Mussolini: "Blood alone moves the wheels of history." Same as it ever was.

No one wins in War except the Military Industrial Complex. A Corporate Cabal run from inside the Pentagon's walls set up to both build weapons of mass destruction and then repair the damage done by them. The astronomical expense of war, at last count $100,000 a minute in maintenance fees, seems paltry when you consider the estimated 37,000 corporations who have their hands in the till and are growing fat on the blood and bones of widows, orphans, and soldiers piling up in mass graves strewn throughout the desert. Oh closer my God to thee!

I pity the fool who prays for life everlasting. I want my taste of Heaven and I want it now. I realize that at any moment I could become the next victim of this War Without End. And Heaven to me would mean dying with a smile on my face screwing half a dozen returning Iraq War veterans. Hell, somebody's gotta take care of the vets. Their own government sure as shit won't. America has over 200,000 homeless veterans of War. Men tossed to the streets and forced to fend for themselves when they were no longer useful as mercenary cogs in the wheel of the world's greatest killing machine; suffering from Post Traumatic Stress Disorder, tricked into a War, and conned by doublespeak into believing that fighting will bring peace, domination will bring freedom, and that your Uncle Sam will take care of you after you've risked life and limb to safeguard his superiority complex.

War is an incurable virus, forever mutating, that travels the globe feeding on man's fear, spreading panic and terror, violence and death. Until we find a vaccine that finally inoculates the entire population against stupidity, arrogance, aggression, and blind faith, we will be forced to forever repeat this War cycle like stunted victims of Orwell's Memory Hole.

PART III

SHORTCHANGED

THE BEAST

He came from Cleveland where the high rate of alcohol poisoning, drug abuse, and teenage suicide cemented his position as a lifelong contender for the F-ward at Bellevue. His parents sent him to NYC to commit him to an institution that could deal with the type of entertainment that he liked to indulge himself in. Like threatening to throw his baby brother out the window of the twenty-first story of the freshly painted suburban high-rent condominium that Mom and Pop just got through paying off.

An addict by fourteen, he had already been diagnosed as dangerous and a threat to society since becoming an active member in several schools practicing sadomasochistic rituals which he would employ against himself and anyone else within spitting distance.

I met him one night on the Bowery when I tried stamping out a fire he had started by giving a homeless man a hot foot. Arguing that it wouldn't be long before he and the bum traded places, I tried reasoning in favor of salvaging the human wreck smoldering on the sidewalk. Hearing nothing of this, he began screaming at me in a piercing falsetto, "I am the Beast . . . 666 . . . *Puta! Puta diablo!*" (I would soon come to recognize this as his mantra.) All the while dancing around me like an evil troll attempting to torch my beautiful auburn locks with a Bic lighter wielded as one would a blowtorch.

I tried wrestling the Beast to the ground with a series of damaging elbow smashes. He began giggling hysterically, drooling and coughing, spewing liquored spitulets all over my face and neck. Disgusted by his rancid breath and inflamed by his atrocious behavior, I retaliated by chewing up a big wad of Oreo cookies mixed with Jack Daniel's and splattering it across the front of his white wife beater.

He dove into me, knocking us both into the side of an oncoming Cadillac, which came to a screeching halt. A drunken Native American with a speech impediment barreled out of the driver's side laughing with delight at what he mistook for a lovers' quarrel. He insisted that me and my newfound wrestling tag-team partner get in—shouting, "What you two need is a little cruise! Hey, how, how, how 'bout taking a ride with me up to, up to, up to Central Park . . . I gotta see a man about a horse!" Laughing at his own banality as he slapped at his skinny thigh.

Always on the prowl for somebody more fucked up than me to pick on, pulverize, or pervert, and never able myself to pass up forward motion, movement, speed, or sleaze, I barrel into the backseat dragging the drunken dwarf with me as some kinda prophylactic against my own disease.

We pull over to piss up against the piers along the West Side Highway, lighting a joint and kicking back some Jack, when a gang of beautiful, queeny Puerto Rican rent boys start rallying round to "check out the freaks"—a mad middle-aged Choctaw Indian, hair almost down to the crack of his ass, sporting low-slung hip-huggers, flip-flops, and love beads, doing a rain dance on the gravel; a squat escapee from Bellevue, Hitler haircut, holes in shoes, almost passing out while pissing on the hood of the Caddy, dick sticky and still dribbling the spent alcohol; and *me*.

Three of the older, harder queers come sauntering over, looking me up and down while snickering, "Ohhh . . . Miss Rough Trade . . . Are you pimping? Or pulling?" A dirty-blonde with razor burns introduces her/himself by lifting up a short spandex skirt and proudly displaying a juicy well-shaved asshole while shouting out the menu of the day. Blowjobs going for a truly competitive five dollars a pop. They start bickering amongst themselves about prices and talents and specialties of the house . . . and who will do what to who if she don't back up . . . and "Hey, Tonto, you got five bucks for me, Big Daddy?" and "Bitch . . . you better watch yourself—I saw him first . . ." And on and on. And what five dollars can buy. And what you can do for five dollars. How with five dollars you can help them, that's right, help them to try and buy their way out, bust their way out, past this scum-encrusted fuckhole. This endlessly ugly urban sprawl.

Where the easy way out is usually the quickest way out . . . is usually a one-way ticket to Rikers or Sing Sing or sailing out on the rusty end of a dull knife blade, or a bullet hole or needle tip, far, far away and flying somewhere above all the bullshit and drivel and doublespeak of do-nothing lifelines that are apparently genetic, you know . . . runs in the family that certain type of sickness, that disease, that insanity, profanity, vanity, malnutrition, addiction, co-addiction, insecurity, inability to deal with reality . . .

What the fuck ever "reality" is supposed to mean when you've spent half your life standing in a welfare line or waiting for the next SSI check or at 2 o'clock in the morning sucking off some scurvy john from New Jersey—with poverty and pollution no longer being metaphors for the state, but an indictment against the chronic state of being.

A constant which reminds you always of where you came from . . . where you're going to . . . and where you're never gunna get . . . and you know no matter what you do, what you try to do, no matter what gets done or don't, it ain't gunna save your sweet ass from falling into a bottomless pit—faceless, graceless, and without a trace.

So the only way out is in. Deep, deep inside yourself. You poke holes in your skin. Thinking that if you just had one solid base where you could concentrate the ache, concentrate the pain, so that it wasn't an all-consuming surround that suffocates you from the first breath of day to your last dying day.

And little Hitler wakes up throwing up all over the knees of one of the queens, who goes into hysterics demanding her five dollars for being the human vomit launch, threatening to shit on his forehead if he doesn't pay up, reaching into his pocket trying to wrangle out a five-spot as the Beast cracks the last of the bottle of Jack against the fender, holds the busted end up to the chippy's pretty face, and with a quick snatch-and-grab manages to pull his/her wig off before jumping into the Caddy, jacked up and screaming to the Indian, "Get in! Get in! Get in! Let's get away with the goods!" shaking the rotted wig out the window. And "Take off, go faster, faster, faster! Break the speed limits, the time limits, the

law . . . Run somebody over, run those bitches over . . .
Let's go back and kill 'em! Let me drive . . . Let me drive!
Let me take the fucking wheel . . . I'll show ya how it's
done . . . Drive—goddamn it! Drive! We're standing still!
You gotta catch the fucking breeze . . . I was born to
fucking fly . . ."

And ninety-two miles an hour up Ninth Avenue with
three teenage Puerto Rican bisexual prostitutes throwing
bricks at the back window and the Indian's hiccupping
nervously trying to catch his breath, and Little Hitler,
all pumped up now, starts flipping the finger to an unsuspecting carload of heavy-looking black dudes with a
necklace of donkey teeth hanging off the rearview mirror. Screaming, "Kiss my lily-white ass, you assholes!"
They do a double take, a look of WHAT THE FUCK? on
their mugs as the Beast, a.k.a. Little Hitler, a.k.a. this
fucking asshole next to me, who I was idiotic enough to
jump in a car with starts screaming out racial epithets
soon to be turned into a custom-made obituary. As our
future executioners race up alongside us, one of them
releasing the pressure in his tight black trousers by pulling out a small pearl-handled black-and-white hand-
gun which he starts wagging out the window three feet
from my right temple. And shit for sure I'm shaking and
they're screaming that I "better shut that faggot honkey
ass up . . . Shut him up! Shut him up! What—is he fucking nuts? You wanna die motherfucker, you wanna die?"
And "What kinda cheesy bitch be banging it with low-
life scum?" Didn't I wanna earn a little bit more dime-bag
money? . . . They needed some fresh white meat in their
stable . . . "Check it out, she got some fine white titties!"

Everybody's yelling and gesticulating wildly as we

push the Caddy up to ninety-six miles an hour . . . "Play that Funky Music" blaring on the car radio and the loud-mouth next to me starts howling out "666 . . . I am the Beast! *Puta . . . Puta madre!*" as we're racing up to 110th Street faster than a greased rat's ass blowing every red light, the wrong way up one-way streets for thirty-two blocks, no fucking cops when ya need 'em . . . no fucking cops and we're blasting on the friggin' horn . . . They could have heard us in Hoboken if anyone had been listening, but the whole fucking city was hammering away, hammering away, and we were just a tiny close-up of life about ready to abort itself.

And the closer they get the gun to my face, the wilder the asshole next to me is getting. Cursing the mothers and godmothers of our would-be killers, yelling at them to "Blow our fucking brains out! . . . Go ahead and do it, you chicken-shit all-dick-no-balls black boys . . . What the hell ya waiting for, City Hall? It's two miles in the other direction!" And as the Sicilians are fond of saying, BE CAREFUL WHAT YOU ASK FOR, because no sooner said than done, and they start firing tiny bullets, little pellets which rip into the bloodstain-red interior as the Indian who has now also joined in the fun begins yee-hawing and yippity-dip-do-ing like it's a Wild West comedy fest, stuttering so hard he can barely control the wheel and "666! I am the Beast!" And I'm freaking out trying to convince myself that I'm too stubborn to die . . . too young to die, too goddamn pretty to die . . . And with a sharp right turn we pull up right behind an empty police van and park Kojak-style as if nothing happened while the sharpshooters sail off into the sunset screaming out our license plate.

* * *

[Author's Note: At least once a week for three years running, an equally outlandish adventure cemented my friendship with the Beast until it finally collapsed under the strain of a mutually accelerating frenzy.]

The last time I saw the Beast, he was in St. Vincent's Hospital where they were threatening to amputate his right arm to eliminate the cellulitis, a cancer and rancor, crank-related. He got off easy when they decided to just gut it, leaving a gorgeous scar four inches wide and three centimeters deep running from wrist to armpit, doing gentle swirling twists all the way down the inside of his useless limb. I knew half a dozen guys who would have killed for that type of memento, a souvenir that says FUCK YOU . . . I'm a survivor, if you wanna get rid of me you're gunna have to chop me up in little pieces. And I pictured him a head on a skateboard buzzing down to the men's shelter where he started living after they let him out of St. Vincent's because there were only so many beds and they wouldn't take him back at Bellevue because he no longer qualified as a serious mental health threat or in need of intensive care or could be considered disabled, except for the fact that his motor functions didn't and the chemotherapy left him pallid and weak and he was constantly hallucinating with the fever of delirium caused by the painkillers or by the methadone treatments or the Thorazine or the Xanax and Ritalin, the Percodan and Placidil, the antipsychotics and antidepressants . . . the whatever the hell it was it took to placate him into a permanent sedation, a stupor, a torpor.

And even though they couldn't just lock him up and throw away the keyhole, it wasn't two months later that he was back in detox for the fortieth time, trying to fight the Devil in the bottle and losing badly. Saying, "I need the juice . . . I need the juice . . ." to recharge his battery. It had been overloaded. His circuits went haywire. He short-circuited. It was pure chaos. He was being devoured. His blood flow was quicksand. He was looking for someone, for anyone to break the free fall. He was free-falling into a timeless wonderland where sight and sound were replaced with smell and taste and touch—"AND NOBODY WANTS TO TOUCH ME ANYMORE"—and the only touch is that of a wet hand on the back of his neck like the kiss of death reaching up from under his deathbed.

And the scars on his arm just weren't healing right and more talk of amputation since he couldn't afford the antibiotics after getting kicked out of first the Palace Hotel above CBGB's and then the men's shelter on 4th Street when they found out he had AIDS, so it was back to sleeping on the Bowery which was way worse than Bellevue because at least there you could steal chump change from the other inmates. But in no way was it as bad as being sent to Rikers when he got busted for selling methadone on the corner of 2nd Street and Avenue B, since he had the misfortune of running into the same Puerto Rican fags he puked on at the piers who proceeded to gang-rape him with a crusty Coke bottle requiring twenty-four stitches to close the festering wound. But he was released immediately after surgery and even managed to pick up a trick or two on the way back to the city.

And I'm swallowing this all down staring into his beautiful bloodshot blue eyes and finally gather up the guts to ask him what's taking so long. What's taking so fucking long? What's he holding back for? What is it he's holding on for, holding on to? How many more times does he want to go through this? Does he want to put me through this? How much longer can he show off by showing up with the next murderous dose of no-good-news? How many more daily disasters? How much more devastation, degeneration, can he put himself through? What's he waiting for? Xmas, Easter, his birthday . . . ? Why doesn't he just fucking snuff it . . . go for broke? Why break it up in little pieces? I know he's got it in him . . . It ain't like he ain't got the gall or the balls . . . or that he hasn't been trying to fucking kill himself for every single day since ten years before I even met him . . .

And he looks up at me all watery and wounded and says, "It's because I'm scared. I'm scared . . ." Scared that when he passes on he'll be called up on all the false starts and half-assed attempts and that he'll have to stand in line with his pants down around his ankles and show the world that he was just another picture post-card depiction of a professional loser, all the markings of a two-bit gambler, a petty thief, a hustler, a cheat, a nobody . . . It's nothing *he's* got any control of . . . I mean, it doesn't control *him* . . . It's not that *he's* a victim . . . It's just something that he can't seem to master that wants to master him . . . That seems to master mistakes and disillusion and dementia and, like an addiction to adrenaline, it keeps forcing him to draw and cross that thin blue line dividing reality from insanity . . . safety from harm, right from wrong again. And c'mon! Any idiot can spit in the eye of the Devil, but few are brave enough to get down on all fours and tongue that fiery hole . . . And he's calling out to me that maybe I don't understand. Maybe I just don't understand. How could anybody understand? It's just a classic case of wrong place, wrong time, right guy.

And the next time I see him he might just be smiling, yeah! Smiling on a mountain top counting the corpses of all the young and old alike who didn't know that when the time is right there'll be no time left for whining, for crying, for self-pity. No time left for any more big fights or fuck-ups or handouts. No more corrosive sensation in the limbs, no more muscles as if twisted and being torn, then laid open, bare. No more brittle feeling of being made of glass, no more wincing or cringing at any quick movement or sound. No more unconscious incoherence of steps, of gestures. No more overwhelming central fatigue. And "I'm holding it together by sheer willpower. Holding it all together by sheer willpower!" He was trying to create a void so that I could progress. He was offering the expanse of an impossible space someplace deep inside that would germinate like a generator, sucked into life, sucked into death.

And kill yourself already! . . . All you who are desperate and you who are tortured in body and soul. Lose all hope! There is no more relief for you in this world. The world dances on your graves. All you lucid madmen, the consumptives, the cancer-ridden and plague-stricken, you will be forever misunderstood. There is a point in you that no doctor will ever understand and that is the point which, for me, saves you and makes you majestic. Pure. Marvelous. You are outside of life. Above life. You have pains which the ordinary man will never know. You go beyond and then beyond again and this is why other men are against you. You are poisoning their quietude. You are dissolvers of their stability. You have irrepressible pains, un-resolvable agonies, pains beyond thought which are neither in the body nor in the soul, but which belong to both. The essence of which makes you unadaptable to any known state.

And as for me . . . I participate in your ills and ask you—who dares to measure the tranquilizer for me? In the name of what su-perior light soul to soul can you ever understand me—or expect me to understand you? You who are at the very root of knowledge and clarity—all on account of your insistence . . . our persistence in suf-fering. We whose pain forces a journey into our souls in search of a calm place to cling to. In search of stability in evil, as others search for it in good. We aren't crazy. We know the necessary doses to calm the insatiable sensibilities of the ruptured soul. The trial and error of terror as tranquilizer from which lesser mortals would flee scream-ing. But still we are not committing suicide—why?

And two weeks later he was dead and they held some stinking lousy memorial that none of his real friends went to. That I didn't go to either because I don't get along very well with professional mourners, being one myself. I'm always getting into fights at funerals. No one wants to hear that none of us expected to see thirty anyway and now that a lot of us aren't, everybody's whining and crying about those who were the first to go. AND FUCK IT! If you aren't ready to die every other second of every third day, then you aren't really living. *Because to know about LIFE we have surrounded ourselves with DEATH. With the dead and dying. With the dope fiends, drug addicts, sex fanatics, alcoholic under-achievers, the thieves and prostitutes, the dropouts and deadbeats, and all the misfits who didn't belong, didn't want to belong to any clique or coven or cult. Who by no accident or freak of nature got chosen to be called up . . . like they always knew they* would. Which is why they glutinized and devoured and eventually choked to death on a life that raced forward faster than a speeding bullet.

By simply suppressing drugs or sex you won't suppress the need for crime, the cancers of the body or of the soul, the propensity for despair, inborn stupidity, the frailty of the instincts. You won't be able to stop souls from being predestined for poison, whatever kind that may be. The poison of isolation, of onanism, of deep-rooted weakness. The poison of alcohol, of an antisocial nature. There are souls that are incurable and lost to the rest of society. If you take away from them one means of madness, they will invent ten thousand others. They will create means more insidious, more furious, absolutely desperate. Nature herself is antisocial. Let the lost get lost. They are lost by nature. And all the ideas of moral regeneration won't do anything about it. There is an innate determinism, an indisputable incurability about suicide, crime, idiocy, madness. There is an invincible cuckoldom of man, a fallout of character. There is castration of the mind. Hell is already of this world and there are men who are unhappy runaways destined to repeat their escape eternally.

No one cries for the dead. They cry for themselves . . . those living through death. We, who in our own individual pain, replay the same horrifying scenes in subways and tenements and nightclubs and bars and baths in this blood-soaked necropolis where night fatigue and the hint of catastrophe make sex without secretions seem almost unbearable in this the age of the death of seduction—where the pleasure palaces have been turned into torture chambers in this, the killing zone of false memory.

[Author's note: The Beast was Bradley Field, drummer for Teenage Jesus. This piece thieves such an incredible amount of philosophy from Antonin Artaud's "General Security: The Liquidation of

Opium" that I hereby implicate myself in the commission of criminal plagiarism. Deal with it. Now go and read the original text.]

JOHNNY BEHIND THE DEUCE

You can't save anyone from themselves. You will lose everything by attempting to play savior. You will never heal the wounded. You cannot repair the damage already done by selfish parents, vicious ex-lovers, child molesters, tyrants, poverty, depression, or simple chemical imbalance.

You can't undo psychic wounds, bandage old scars, kiss away ancient bruises. You can't make the pain go away. You can't shout down the voices in people's heads.

You can't make anyone feel special. They will never feel beautiful enough, no matter how beautiful they are to you. They will never feel loved enough, no matter how much you adore them.

You will never be able to save the battered from battling back at a world they've grown to hate. They will always find a way to pick up where the bullies have left off. They will in turn become bullies. They will make you the enemy. They will always find a new method in which to punish themselves. Thereby punishing you. No matter how much you've convinced yourself that you have done absolutely everything in your power to prove your undying devotion, unfaltering commitment, and unending encouragement, you will never be able to save a miserable bastard from himself.

The wounded will always find a way to spread their pain over a vast terrain like an emotional tsunami which devastates the surrounding landscape. An ever-expanding firewall which will singe everything and everyone in its wake. The longer you love a damaged person the more it will hurt you. They will mock your generosity, abuse your kindness, expect your forgiveness, try your patience, sap your energy, and eventually kill your soul. They will not be happy until you are as miserable as they are. Then their incredible self-loathing will be justified by the perpetuation of a cycle from which there is little recourse.

Once you enter their free fall, it will be virtually impossible to turn your back on them. You will be racked with guilt, frustrated by your own impotence, and made furious for ever buying into their bullshit in the first place. Of course, the more damaged, the more charismatic. The more brilliant. The more sexually intoxicating. The more dangerous to your own mental health.

I have spent months, possibly years, comatose on park benches, tracking the periphery of playgrounds, skulking through shopping malls, falling asleep in the library, trying to capture and trap a fleeting image. The image of a young boy, at just the right moment in his life, that transient fleeting second when an incandescent light falls on the hollows of his cheeks, a splash of sun dances on his lips, and that blossom of purity etched deep within his innocent smile rebirths something in me that was lost long ago.

There's something about how fine their bones are. Under their flesh. The possibility of shattering them under my need. Skin pulled tight around bony joints. The flattering reflection of my own beauty divorced of disease, my multiple sicknesses, a withering-away abated. Transformed into a healing tonic, a sexual salvation, vacation from the devastation that has ringed the wellspring of my life.

Not that I could ever forget how much of my life has already been melted away. How much I gave up, gave over, wasted. How much has already been stolen. Destroyed. You don't have to fight yourself too hard to fall in love at least for half an hour, twenty minutes, two days, a week, with a young boy who finds in you the love they never found in their own mother's arms. And reciprocates it twofold. I'll play Mommy. I need to and I'm good at it. There's nothing to lose, and what it is you gain is their life force, a transformation, resurrection, a reckoning, a day off from playing wet nurse in the trauma unit nursing damaged junkies back to health.

But I'm too far gone now, too fucked up, too ill spent to really carry through. Shot to shit and forced to struggle against it. Broken down, battered. Used too much up. Nothing left inside my angel's saving graces, that busted little cherub with dirty feet and greasy wings whose tender ruby-rich kisses have resuscitated so many burning embers and dying remains that I have become a mortician's reanimator, stuck forever in a purgatory that so many dying men have come to rub their poison against.

Even my breath has become toxic. An aerosol taint of glue, sugar water, paint fumes, dead roses, and runoff. But young boys don't know that yet. Don't see it, can't smell my true essence over the sweat of their own passion. Over the smell of their own vinegar, saltwater taffy, dirty towels, steam heat. They wouldn't recognize it even if they did. They have no reference point. No landmarks. No track record. No wars below their belt.

No idea what it's like to inhabit this fleshy prison of blood and bones, as if entombed in an unnamed Nuremberg cathedral which forty years later still remains swept to the side of a blood-stained street, the bones of her confessional stacked helter-skelter, shattered under the steel rods, the rebar of the enemy pilot jets who blew in one day with the taste of her death on their breath, and in their wake, there she still stands, torn to little pieces, praying to be glued back together again. Praying for resurrection, for redemption. Praying with blind faith and stupid adoration to a cruel and vindictive god that does not exist, that one day the wounds will heal over. That a dark angel will tumble down from the heavens, your name on his lips, and with a single kiss, the multiple fractures where memory and madness commit soul murder will cauterize. Will mend. Dissolve. But as with most prayers, I'm wasting my fucking breath.

I fell into his hollow, the vacuum in his eyes, that empty space inside, where beyond his obvious pain, trauma, tragedy, a little boy had long ago been murdered. Butchered. Bludgeoned. Massacred. Left abandoned on some shit-stained road, marked not on any map, but well-defined enough to read in braille.

And it was written all over Johnny. *Dead End. Do Not Enter. End of the Road. Cul-de-sac. No Outlet. Lost Highway.* I should have known better. I *did* know better. I just couldn't stop myself.

Johnny bruises a tender ache inside of me. Even after an all-night bender when he comes swaggering back to my bunk, bent on an ugly kind of drunk, stinking of Wild Irish Rose, sporting another black eye and limping again, the way his face lights up when he knows I'm half awake, been waiting up staring down the clock, sucking up caffeine and codeine, worried sick and swollen from not enough sleep, and pissed off, yeah, pissed, but still thrilled, can't fake it, I just want a kiss, and he gets to live another day, so I get to live another day, which is all the reason I need to forgive him, at least for now.

Because I can't face the fucking fact that one day I may have to live without him, and that day may come sooner than either of us want to admit, but for today, for right now, which is all that matters, he wasn't set up and offed in some two-bit hustle, didn't play patsy to a sleazy pickup line whispered under the breath of a serial-killing sex stalker, he didn't stumble into a speeding car before passing out and pissing all over himself . . . He didn't fall off a fire escape trying to jimmy open and pry out one of the frail old sex queens from a ratty roach-infested bed set on fire in an opium haze by a lit cigarette dropped from the limp fist of some young trick he got dope, dick, and the drips off of . . .

Which he almost did, fall five stories that is, from the roof of the shitbag hotel he night watches, said he didn't even try to catch himself, didn't care, was ready to curse Creation and kiss the concrete, just to see how many bones would shatter, and how bad it would feel when they did, but his belt got looped around a broken rung and instead of wringing his neck, it saved his ass. And that was just last week.

"If I was a soldier, I'd trip over a land mine," he

laughs, small belly chuckle, eyes not faking too hard an innocence he still manages to maintain, and with all my might, try as I do, I just can't decode how . . .

But the beauty is, Johnny doesn't get it either, doesn't see it, can't feel it, so busy dousing his wounds with Betadine, counting his scars, picking at scabs, another hairline fracture here, a small concussion there, bloody rags wrapped around the temple, soaking up the fallout from the body as battlefield to be trampled under by his big black boots . . .

Storm troopers kicking the shit out of the enemy within, waging counteroffensives which will guarantee mutually assured destruction not only against himself, not only against me, but aimed directly at the shell-shocked and battle-fatigued little boy who screams for ceasefire in the bunker and wants his mother to kamikaze in to the demilitarized zone . . .

That unchartered territory where a part of him still lives, the part that cowers in the far corner late at night, scared of shadows and holy ghosts, scared of losing life before figuring out exactly what it means to fucking live, and his life is an endless barrage of bullshit and petty disasters, where losing whatever it is you're desperately trying to hold on to is not only natural but almost genetically preprogrammed, and Jesus Christ, I want to save him from himself, want to take care of him, mother him, love him, get him to love himself, be saint, savior, and favorite sin, but we're both sick with need, sick on each other, and not a single day goes by that I don't whisper a stupid prayer that smears God's name to keep him safe. But he's not safe. He's not safe. He's not safe from me. And I'm not safe from him.

* * *

Johnny crawls into bed bloody and beer-stained. He's cut himself again. I pretend I'm still sleeping. He feels closer to me, safer, he relaxes when I'm half dead. He cradles into my coma. It calms him down, slows his blood. He presses himself against me. His thick leather belt sweats against my back. He buries his face in my hair. Inhales slowly. Supping on my dusky aroma, a dirty-white honeysuckle stained with night's runoff. I am the oxygen he feeds upon. A cleansing hallucinogen, the undercurrent of musky heat radiates life into his open mouth. When he's with me he can breathe again.

I feel his excitement building. The air catches fire in his dry cottony throat. He swallows, mouths, *I want so bad to love you like you pretend to love me.* I tremble. Not moving. Frozen like a still frame cracked and trapped inside a broken movie projector.

I want so bad to lash out, thrash against him, scream his name. Pound his temples. Smash him in the face. Shoot him in the fucking head. Stab his lower lip, his arms, his legs, his back and chest, cut him into a thousand crimson ribbons so that he would, for that one moment, truly comprehend just how much I do love him. How badly I want him, how needy I really am. How hungry. How incredibly moist.

Tucking himself into me, a fleshy surround. I submit to his filthy electric force field and fold myself under him. Into him. My body seems to dissolve, shrink, condense, and unfold into a small pocket, hollow pillow, pussy willow soft, which he blankets in dusty skin. The 147 self-inflicted scars on his chest and arms are cool pink fingers which mouth my surrender. I have no resistance left, not an ounce, once they press up against me. Skin sliced to the bone. Brilliant. Because it defines so well the pain we both share, but can never, either of us, ever admit to.

Johnny doesn't start violent, but I know that's how he'll finish me off. Finish himself off. He knows I want him to hurt me. I need to be hurt. Need to be reminded how much he loves me. Loves me enough to hurt me even though he hates me for wanting it. Hates me for what I do to him, make him do to me. Hates me because he needs to hurt himself too, and now I am the most available tool.

But first, his soft wet lips, sweeter even than a virgin's pouting mound, surprise the back of my neck. Disappear into collar bones. Crawl up into my hair. He inhales, sucking in a fistful of auburn locks. His tenderness is made so much more desperate, delicious, cruel, by where I know he'll take me. How he'll take me. How far he'll push it. How far he needs to go.

He can't resist much longer. If I exhale a certain amount of breath . . . when my rib cage rises and falls into the light and shadow of early-morning exhaust . . . and the air jet streams from my mouth signaling a passive languor, that's when he'll pounce. He stuffs his fingers in his mouth. Small sucking sounds. I still don't move. His left hand dances down my spine. His right pulls my panties aside. They cut into my thigh. Scald the fleshy inside. With surgical skill he spreads me open, so slowly I can barely feel the pressure of skin separating, flowering. It's only the influx of moist body heat which signals the stretching of succulent meat. He slips two fingers inside me. Inching up to the last knuckle. Taut resistance. Gentle spasm. He's in my ass, that glorious masterpiece, the maker's most temperamental vestibule. Pressing against me from behind, he's getting hard, a fallen angel, blessing me with the salvation of his sex.

He still thinks I'm asleep. Removes his fingers long enough to smell and lick. Sticks them back in. Takes them out again. Smells and licks. He's now too hard to resist my fragrant blossom. He's forcing himself in. Massive expansion of tender cubby. I'm stuffed to bursting, terrified. But no time to contemplate the consequences. The clock's gone haywire. He's suddenly impatient. Rough. He shoves one hand over my mouth. I can taste my almond musk.

"This is what you want, isn't it . . . isn't it? Tell me how much you want it, tell me how much you want my cock, tell me, baby, you know you want it . . . tell me," he threatens under his breath. Thrashing against me. Pumping fingers down my throat. Glued like a puppet on a flesh stick.

Then I see it. Out of the corner of my eye. Steel tip glint. I hear his skin rip. Deep crimson incision. Small audible shudder. Slight smile. Sweet kiss. Another laceration to his chest, under his collar bone. Flesh tone turns fatty pink then deep scarlet. Eight or nine inches of thick syrup flows down his chest in bloody rivulets. Cakes around the base of his dick. Trickles onto and tickles his balls. Hot dribble drives his delirium. Can't stop himself now from banshee bucking. Fury fucking the drippy dry glue into the base of my spine from the outside in.

Lubricated with his browning blood, my delicate camellia revolts and tightens, almost tearing, searing

itself on his poisoned heat flow. Pummeling me senseless, there is no recourse other than to meet his thrusts
with equal dementia. Sticky and slick turns gummy and
thicker still. Hideous swell. Horrible explosion. Mutual expulsion. He jackhammers the last few droplets of
come and blood into my hollow. Squashed under him, I
collapse. Feel myself drain, deflate. He ebbs out slowly.
Gagging for air.

But there is no air. It's too thick to breathe. The
swampy atmosphere is stained with spunk and plasma.
Johnny burrows into the small of my back. Tickling, licking, lapping at my oozing wound. His lips and tongue
bathing my bruise. "We're both bleeding . . ." he baby
talks.

I had been running the straight-and-narrow for as long
as I could remember. For no good reason other than
loneliness hit harder while nursing a hangover. A brain-
crushing headache and sour stomach became a tiring
way to greet the day. Then came Johnny.

Not that I could blame him for my multiple indiscre-
tions. It just made sloppy easier, more seductive to slip
back into. Felt almost criminal crawling around on all
fours neck deep in the murky undertow. Dwell inside of
someone else's psychic surgery for a while. It felt good
to just let myself dissolve. Binge and purge. Choke on
excess and suffer the consequences. Not give a shit. Be
selfish. Greedy. Disappear into need. Submerge in desire. Crash, get jacked up, and crash again. Johnny and
I started getting lubed on coke every weekend. Glut on
Friday and Saturday night. Reel and feel like shit until Tuesday or Wednesday. Fuck ourselves out. Spasm

into conversations that would begin at midnight and dwindle down hours later, long after the dawn had been blanketed over by dirty sheets that blocked out the sun.

The ritual always began the same. Hack out enough lines to force into cardiac arrest lesser mortals. Preparation for evaporation into a secret place. An undulating womb, which would expand and contract as the walls fell in upon themselves crushing out our breath. Our moods swung to whatever song was playing. Jump-cutting from blues to bebop to trance. Like our mind-set. A distorted juke box cranked full of musty tunes you could almost sing along to, but the melody kept escaping just as you got to the second verse.

Five hours into another Friday-night binge. Slinking into the lull between rushes. A moment of spastic paralysis as the muscles still tremble but the outer shell of the body freezes, locked into an electric rigor mortis.

Johnny was on the couch, one hand grabbing his bulge, the other playing spin-the-bottle with a broken fifth whose busted mouth reflected a smoky golden haze that meant we'd be screwing through another fractured day. I needed to wipe the dribble from my upper lip, comb my hair, grab a coat, search for my keys, and then try to remember how to drive, so I could rescue enough libations to see us through until the spell wore off and we were finally able to pass out in each other's arms again, brittle but still greedy. Couldn't send Johnny. He didn't drive. Couldn't send him even if he did. Didn't trust him. Not in his state.

Tiny's Tight Spot was the only place that would sell after hours. Scuzzy flop on the far end of downtown where only the lifers and ex-cops went to booze. Been paying off the precinct captains in the fifth ward for decades with free drinks, grilled bologna sandwiches, and 150 bucks a week. Stayed in business with what they did under the table. Shots were still fifty cents a round. Had to protect the regulars. Some occupied the same bar stool for forty years running. Three-quarters of a mile going twenty-five should've put me there and back in about fifteen minutes.

I placed my order with Tony, the owner. Two six-packs of Schlitz, Johnny's favorite, and an overpriced fifth. Grabbed the bag and split.

A slice of dirty brown was shredding a crack in the horizon. The electricity bouncing off the streetlights made everything look hollow. Ghostly. Life-sized images of what real once was. I was no longer sure I knew. My high was folding, crumbling. I reached across the seat to pet the paper bag, praying the booty of firewater would by proxy rekindle a small flare-up in Johnny's loins. I'd be back home in a matter of minutes, where I could throw my arms around his neck, slip my tongue in his mouth, and breathe. I was halfway through the intersection before I saw the squad car. Too late to stop, I simply played good citizen and pulled over. Routine bullshit. License, registration, insurance.

"Where you headed?"

"Home."

"What's in the bag?"

"Schlitz and Jack Daniel's . . . Fancy a shot?"

"Turn off the ignition."

"Is that really necessary?"

"Do it. And get out of the car. Hands on the hood."

Believe it or not, I know when to quit. Did what was expected. Got out of the car. Typical traffic stop, but with a twist. Everyone was under suspicion now that the Bank Street Boys, a notorious gang of teenage hustlers, were turning up facedown in the Gratz River. Dead bodies were hitting double digits. Downtown hood rats scurried home after dark, turning bored traffic cops into Bad Lieutenants. Tried to make small talk just to distract the bull from looking too close into my pinwheel eyes, runny nose, nervous condition. Not that they'd suspect a woman. Women don't kill for no reason. When a woman murders, it's usually a crime of passion—lover, ex-boyfriend, husband. Not a pack of prostitutes. That's man's work, right? Killing off over and over again, the replicons of their first, their last, their ever-present rejection. Killing again and again, their lousy mother, the haughty cheerleader who snubbed them in tenth grade, the prom queen who at the last minute went to the dance with the football hero, the night nurse, the convenience store clerk, the women who represented to their tortured libidos all those who wouldn't give it up before, but were selling it off in little chunks now, to anyone who could afford it . . . That's what Bundy and Speck and Ramirez did. That's not what women do. But that's just the coke talking, so I keep it to myself and nod like a good girl, hoping all my papers check out and I won't have to give this creep my mouth, just so I can hurry home to Johnny, who I'll have to suck back up again after being gone now for a good forty-five minutes anyway.

Officer O'Riley, or McKenna, or O'Rourke, or whatever the hell his smudgy badge reads, gets an APB on his car radio as I'm ruminating on my serial killer psychobabble, and without so much as a spit of dismissal, hops in the front seat of his cruiser and speeds off. Good thing. Because I was starting to scare myself. Wondering just how many ounces his Smith & Wesson clocked in at, and just how fast I'd need to be to get away with kicking him once in the nuts, poking him in the eye, grabbing his gun and firing off a round or two, hopping back in my shitty spitfire, and riding the gas all the way back home to that hunky fuck who by now was probably passed out.

I could hear Johnny's panicked ranting before the key was in the lock. Feel the vibration of boots cracking against the door. He'd take two steps forward, check the peephole, kick the door frame, take two steps back, and repeat. He flung the door open with such force he fell backwards and landed on his ass. Sprung up like a coiled rattler, ripe with venom.

"HA! I knew it was you . . . Where the fuck have you been?"

"Hey, slow down, tiger, I was out getting drinks, remember?"

He towered over me, insisting I look him in the eye. His were red and bulging, dirty tears now dried, streaking his cheeks. A new three-inch laceration over left eyebrow, ruby-red and congealing. A bloody smudge under his left nostril. Caked with coke. Neck ringed with sweat. Wet hair framing his contorted face. Lips cracked and chapped. Beautiful and psychotic. Ripped to shit and gone.

"Well, what the fuck took you so long? Did you blow the fucking bartender for a six-pack?"

"What???"

This shit came out of nowhere. Forty-seven minutes ago we were playing piggy in the throws of a lust
which bordered on pornographic. Now he's pissed that
I bought HIM beer? I didn't get it.

"Johnny . . . that's ridiculous . . . c'mon . . . cool out.
Have a drink." I reached up to pull his face closer. He
slapped my hand away.

"NO!!!" he bellowed.

I headed toward the kitchen, pulling out a tall boy as
peace offering, but he was just warming up.

"Don't fucking walk away . . . Answer me!" He spun
me around, grabbed the collar of my coat, and pulled
it down to my waist. Manic. "You fucking whore . . . I
knew it. Look at you. Since when do you go out for beer
in the middle of the goddamn night with just a slip on
under your coat? You smell like you were fucking the
whole bar, you cunt."

"Are you tripping? I went to the bar flying out of my
gourd to get you some fucking beer. On the way back
I got pulled over. If the fucking cops hadn't gotten another call, I'd be sucking on a Breathalyzer downtown
right now. What the fuck is up with *you?*"

I pulled away pissed. Started toward the fridge,
passing the coffee table we used as altar for the ceremo-
nial ritual of our drugged communion. It was tipped on
its side. Broken glass, ashes, cigarette butts scattershot
on the couch and floor. Baggies torn apart at the seam.
Blood-smeared straw orphaned on the saucer, which had
been licked clean. The last of our stash, a hundred bucks
worth, sucked up while I was gone. I was furious.

He trailed after me. "We need more coke. Call your
dealer. See if he'll come by."

"Are you nuts? It's 7 in the fucking morning, you're tweaked, and we just ripped through 250 bucks worth. Do I look like fucking Noriega?"

"I need more fucking coke . . . I mean it . . . I'm on to something here. Crystallized thought. Sharp as ice. I need to ride this out. Everything's just starting to make complete sense. The body as Experimental Canvas, the body as Blood Bank, as Punching Bag, Carving Board, Sack of Pus and Come. Don't cut me off now. Give me his number. If you don't want to call him, I will." He picked up the phone, raced over to me. Smiling. "Please, baby, please." Grinning like a twelve-year-old suffering from chronic dementia.

"I WILL NOT CALL HIM! You're out of your fricking mind. They don't deliver on credit, remember? Have a goddamn beer and cool it."

"I WILL NOT COOL IT! GIVE ME THE NUMBER! GIVE ME THE NUMBER! GIVE ME THE NUMBER!" Kicking holes in the wall with his size-thirteen steel tips.

"NO! Calm the fuck down. You're losing it!" I ran over to him, grabbed one arm behind his back, landed a nerve pinch between his neck and shoulder blade, which dropped him to his knees, and using my full body weight, shoved him head first into the pile of cigarette butts and broken beer bottles.

"Oww! Cut that shit out!"

Right. Okay for him to turn asshole, break up my shit, insult my generosity, and demand I cater to HIM, but fucking forbid the little bitch to give him a taste of his own poison. He starts to freak.

"Fuck you, Johnny . . . You're way out of line here. Shut up, settle down, or get the fuck out. Now."

"Fine, you bitch. I'm going out. Piss off." He stumbles to his feet, flips me off sticking out his tongue, pretends to straighten his filthy clothes, yanks open the front door, and falls flat on his face screaming his ex-wife's name.

Johnny could stubbornly avoid sleep for forty-six, sixty-eight, seventy-two hours at a time. Propelled by alcohol, speed, coke, adrenaline, or just sheer panic, he'd string himself so far out he could barely light a cigarette. Raise a bottle. Trembling hands massaging a leg spasm. Chapped lips cracked by pointy canines. X-ray eyes detecting invisible monsters who'd steal him from me as he night-stalked energy trails, falling stars, fading headlights, meteors, night birds, stray cats. Flashlight cocked to hip, butcher knife in torn back pocket. Sneak-peeping around corners. Frozen in door frames. Glued to the window sill, peeking through a cigarette burn in the fabric. Paralyzed at the foot of the stairs. Paranoid agitation strangled the hours. Fueled his psychosis. Bored the shit out of me.

Forcing me into silence, he attempted to decode the flow of traffic two blocks away, the scampering of rats in the next building, an ant hill under construction in the backyard. An insane reconnaissance mission. The enemy . . . a sonic surround. Every creaky floorboard, rattling pipe, electrical hum, a forged television static which seemed to leak from his ears out. Filling the room with a reverberating symphony of subdecibel tones only he could hear. A swelling claustrophobia. The cold sweat on his brow expanding like a freak weather pattern which coated the room in a dense fog of atmospheric perspiration.

Sex became impossible. Johnny couldn't focus. I'd be curled around him, one leg snaked high up on his hip, wiggling against him. He'd be teasing me with cool fingers, tickling my inner thighs, whispering about the texture of my flesh. How its plump satin was as sweet as honeyed butter. To be suffocating there, buried alive, inhaling my heat, was heaven, the only place he felt safe. Home. I'd cry for him to take me, give me more, feed it to me, finish me off, do something, anything, More. Please. Now.

A car door would slam halfway up the block. He'd jump out of bed, mute the stereo, turn off all the lights, run to the window. Jimmy it open a crack to get a better look. He'd weave like a punch-drunk boxer attempting to spy a crack in the darkness through which he could narrow his vision in order to locate the intruder. He'd go through this routine six or seven times a night. Sentry at his post for countless hours. Waiting for the imaginary invader to materialize. Forever convinced that whoever was out to get him, for whatever reason, was sure to eventually appear, pull up right in front of my apartment, kick the door in, and take him away. No amount of practical reasoning would sway his dedication to this bizarre night watch. I assumed it was a hangover from digging the graveyard shift at the shitty hotel he used to work at. Try to convince him of that. He wouldn't hear it. Eventually I'd grow bored, begin to fume, leave the room. Frustrated. Pissed off. Dejected.

His paranoia battered my resolve. The end whimpered in like a small sick breeze one spring night. We were laying on the couch softly purring into each other's mouth. So worked up and wet, the cushions were sticky.

He was on top of me, his beautiful face inches away from mine, eyes half closed, lips parted just enough for the tip of his tongue to taste my breath. I blew in his mouth. He inhaled a whisper of moist heat. Blew it back at me. Light kiss. Bliss. Dreamscape. Dissolve. And the sound of small claws scampering up on the roof. Raccoons in heat. Such was the season. Johnny bolted off of me, wild-eyed, panicked. Pulling at his hair, his eyebrows and lips, muttering, "I knew those fuckers would come back! Bastards. Where's the knife? Where's the fucking buck knife? Hurry up get the knife!"

"What bastards? Who's come back?" Bewildered. Drained.

"The assholes who've been taping me! I know they're taping our conversations. I saw them in a black van last week. Cameras, tape recorders. Parked out front. They're back! And now they're on the roof . . . Shit!"

"They are not on the goddamn roof. Get a fucking grip on yourself! It's probably just a squirrel. A fucking raccoon."

We had been through this before. A week earlier.

Four in the morning. I had forced him out of bed and led him by the hand to stand across the street from my apartment, arguing for two and a half hours about the construction of the roof. Unable to assure him that it was slanted to such a degree that no human being had the dexterity to dance, walk, run, or climb upon its slanted gables. He was not convinced.

"Yeah . . . well, raccoons don't sit in vans shoving a microphone out the side window, do they? DO THEY?"

"What the hell are you talking about?"

"SHHHH! Can't you hear that?"

"Yeah, I do . . . and if it was human, and it heard us making a fricking racket, don't you think he'd split?"

"I'm calling the cops!"

"No you're not! Are you nuts? There's drugs all over this house. They'll take one look at you and call for an ambulance."

"Where's the phone? Where's the goddamn phone?"

Johnny flipped the pillows off the couch, turned the chairs over, knocked the TV off the shelf, checked his back pocket and my purse in search of the phone. Finding it finally, where it always was—on the kitchen counter—and stupidly dialing 911. I snatched the phone away to hang it up, calling him a fucking idiot. It rings in my hand. He grabs it back, conspiratorially whispering to the operator, who by law will respect penal code section 13730 and dispatch a squad car, "It's you, isn't it? The guy in the black van? I knew it was you . . . I knew it!"

"Johnny behind the Deuce" was originally conceived as a film treatment which was generously financed by Gregg Hale, best known as producer of The Blair Witch Project.

DEAR JOHNNY, JIMMY, JOEY, FRANKIE, MARTY, TONY, TOMMY . . .

Beautiful liar. Blood-sucking junkie. Baby-faced killer. Serial rapist. Lecherous pedophile. Thief, con, crook, cunt. Derelict bastard cock-sucking cunt slut.

Fuck you, death-defying mortifier. Night-stalking my graveyard. I opened the casket of my tomb, and with my last dying breath I spent myself of all perfume, my night-blooming jasmine, my gardenia, the magnolia of my youth, pulled up by the roots, tender shoots . . . pissed upon. Again. By you.

How fucking dare you . . .

Bottomless vacuum, endless gully, empty black soul hole. The center of a parasitic universe. You have leeched me of all sensation. All emotion. Sucking on my life force in a cannibalistic feeding frenzy that has bled the color from my skin, the blood from my bones.

I endlessly allowed you to be the virulent pig you always were, but you resented my generosity when you were drowning in gluttony. I offered up not only my body, which you ravished as disposable playpen, but my very essence, which you were unable to kill with your contagions, but have nonetheless polluted and forever stained with your filthy bloodshed.

Overwhelmingly virulent, you suffocate in a nostalgic surround gagging on ancient wounds whose fumes have now become your poisoned succulent. You feared my elemental magic, mistaking it for bad voodoo which you turned against yourself. Lacerated by beauty, you accused mine of being a covert sabotage that has accelerated your downfall.

I would rather be crushed into mortar, under rock and volcanic ash, pounded into quarry and reduced to sandstone, broken glass, tiny bones like the beaks of small birds, than to be once more swept away, seduced by your brilliant bullshit. You have cast me out, cut me off, and corrupted everything I offered up to you. I am left floating on a sea of toxic magnetic resonance. The by-product of your diseased runoff.

Desperate and destitute, you have dumped my remains in the valley of unrest, unreason. That is where you have taken me. Stranded me. You swore to never leave me, but you left me long ago, night after bitter night while still standing in front of me drunk. Demented with rage, your fear turned to loathing. Accusing me of perpetrating the crimes you only wish you had committed. Dredging through the dregs of my ancient history like an inquisitorial archeologist sifting the sand drifts of all eternity for evidence of my corruption, which in turn you claim has corrupted you. But you came to me contaminated, and I admit it has perverted your ability to reason.

You force an instant replay of the gruesome details of my own life which I can no longer even recall. The high court of your false morality condemns me to the spiral Tourette's of your self-righteous judgment, where I stand forever convicted as the deviant criminal you secretly wish you were.

You insisted my passion was self-serving and hedonistic. My power fascist in nature. My fluidity a ruse to infiltrate. My beauty a curse I used against others to bend them to my will, using my sex to manipulate addiction. My strength was alien. My ability to live outside the disappointing constraints of the world's corrosive stranglehold, fraudulently utopian. My belief in the ability to overcome trauma, proof I was ignorant of your immense and catastrophic pain. The burden of which saints you as martyr, paints me as sinner, and worships at the foot of a false god whose cruelty I can no longer play victim to.

You forced me to play witness to your madness, pounding on temples, smashing in cheekbones, pummeling your beautiful face into a vile monstrosity, until I could no longer look at you. Claiming it retaliation against the living ghosts that haunt you. But you are only haunting yourself. Stalking yourself. Murdering your self. And your death cannot come quick enough. Your protracted slow-motion suicide plays itself out in an endless loop of predictable repetition, a low-budget circus side show steeped in horror which feeds on an audience of one who can no longer afford the admission.

Your death will be more satisfying, more complete, more honest and right than the torture your chronic demise forces me to suffer through. You shat on everything I am, everything I offered you. You have insulted my gifts with a barbarism of unparalleled brutality from which I have now become immune. I extended to you a refuge, a stay of execution, respite. You bombarded my safe haven with chaos, confusion, and a grandiose self-pity which bordered on megalomania, robbing me of everything I once held sacred.

And I can't wait for you to tighten the noose, to pull the fucking trigger, shove the knife far enough inside you that not only do you sever the artery connecting your life to mine, but you snuff out your own life once and for all. Because if you don't kill yourself, I will be forced to kill you.

Beautiful liar. Blood-sucking junkie. Baby-faced killer. Serial rapist. Lecherous pedophile. Thief, con, crook, cunt. Derelict bastard cock-sucking cunt slut. Fuck you. Fuck you. Fuck you. You fuck.

DEAD MAN

The Dead Man slowly rises from the sand pit crawling on all fours out from under forty feet of dry rust. He musters the strength of dead men everywhere who supply him with just enough false energy to pick himself up, dust himself off, and collapse against me. His dead weight crushes me, obliterating all feeling. Squashing sensation. Deadening the senses. Dulling reason. My breath slows. Breathing barely enough to supply oxygen to the brain. Pulse slows, skids, stops. I am paralyzed. I flatline. Time dies. I disappear. Reappear.

I stand directly before him whitewashed by steam heat rippling in off the desert floor. I am merely a mirage, his mirage, which he sees through yet refuses to acknowledge. He fills my body forcing expansion. Occupies every inch of skin and sinew as if I have swallowed an inflatable Death doll. Toxic pressure expands my flesh. He slurs, a sandy murmur, indecipherable and droll. Rocks his head just enough to draw his eyes down. His vision, like a desert rat, doesn't serve much purpose in the blistering mid-afternoon sun whose glorious golden patina cruelly kisses and blisters even that which it does not touch. But his night vision penetrates great distances, piercing the heart of dead stars and black holes. His viridian eyes are cloudy pools of viscous liquid. I am no longer alone here. In my skin. No longer in control.

I move my lips in protest but my breath has turned to dust. My bones are hollow husks. It's all up to him now. Deadpan joker. Pokerfaced. A cheap practitioner of gruesome parlor tricks. Slight of hand. Geomancy. Games of chance. Baccarat. His specialty—a seance of senseless violence. His favorite—Russian Roulette. Using my head for target practice.

I have a soft spot for him. Though the feeling is not mutual. He hates my fucking guts. But he hates everyone and everything even more than he despises me. He merely uses me as puppet vehicle, a truck of flesh to drive his crimes.

Dry whispers. Dead kisses. Lips as thin as paper cuts. Mouthing instructions which I will fight with all my will not to follow: Throw myself under a school bus. A tractor trailer. Into the river. Off the roof of the post office. Into a speeding car. Fall asleep on the train tracks, moonlight leaking through dead leaves. Pick up the snub-nosed .38 Special and blow my left cheek off. Hang from the rafters, dangling on a dirty clothesline used as umbilical cord connecting me to Death.

A cool evening breeze kisses dirty feet, my tongue swollen, preventing argument against his hypnotic pull. His words choke in my throat, a seductive wheezing of parched breath. A lesser mortal would be made weak by his black magic mantra. One less rebellious might acquiesce, overcome by the need to please the person who seems to need nothing. Need no one. Need not even exist in clock time.

For the gravedigger of crushed dreams and false promises, that caretaker of the endless obsidian spiral has a penchant to materialize at random, to disappear for years on end and to reappear when and where you least expect him. His ability to cut a woman in half, in quarters, to watch her splinter, shatter, and dissolve into the dust from whence he comes, only to resuscitate her so she may live and die and live again as her mouth fills with his strangled breath, is testament enough to the dominion he holds over the hoax known as Death's Other Kingdom. For Death must surely be a hoax, a trick, a labyrinth, a secret passage with a hidden switchboard, separated from Life only by our mortal perception of it. For if you believe like I do in the invisibile, the inanimate, the inaudible, the impossible, then no doubt the Dead Man will one day also call your name. I know him well. He is my better half.

THE DEVIL'S RACETRACK:
RAY TRAILER

Prisoner #32578 is shitting himself to death in the next cell. Every twenty minutes another round of bowel-splitting explosions rack his body. He coughs, cries out, pounds his head on the cinder block walls, and wails. The smell is awful. As thick as oatmeal. His impending death from dehydration signals small relief as its horrendous aroma wafts down the hall walloping the senses. Mingling with the already heady fragrance of thousands of spent bladders pissing into eternity since the turn of the century. The smell of old men's fecal remains, their sour and rancid flesh rotting from the inside out, reeks until it stains the interior of your own nasal cavity, forcing you to become one with the smell. A seething odorama contaminated by the decay of hundreds of lost men whose very souls have started to stink.

Pickled feet and dirty fingernails. Silent pleas have been scratched into every surface, deep grooves in the floors, walls, bunks, sinks. An homage to endless days ill spent. Locked inside this human warehouse of disease and petty disasters. Where wasted lives count the days until release, relief, return, or death.

Another notch on the wall to keep you sane . . . keep you insane . . .

On my back in my bunk. A waiting game. Poisoned stalactites hang heavy with a toxic runoff steeped in decades of disappointment. Years of nervous, bored sweat cling to the ceiling and walls. Threatening to drown me. Drip by drip. In the eyes, the nose, the mouth, the ears. Browning like nicotine stains forming a Rorschach test in every corner. Sticky to the touch, foul to behold its ceaseless descent. I pull my T-shirt over my head. At least the smell is my own. Smells like sorrow. Like spoiled meat. Like a beaten man, tricked by his own gullibility. Tricked into believing . . . tricked into someone else's beliefs . . .

I close my eyes and meditate. Fooling myself, with all of my will, into summoning Her smell. I breathe slowly, deeply, inhaling my own aroma, a bittersweet stench whose undercurrents with much torque of the imagination are magically transformed into Hers. Into what I remember of Her. I will never forget Her. The scent that emanates from the small of Her back. The smell of butter. Clove. Coffee. Cayenne. A spicy, pungent fragrance whose mysterious depths sting with intrigue. Rebellion. Deception. A perfume so steeped in magic that a mere mortal's most strident resolve disintegrates once intoxicated by the ether of its undertones. A perfumed poison whose fragrance scrambles the synapses. Turns men into obedient little puppies whose only wish is to please the Bitch Goddess. The witch whose wanton desires manifest themselves in a catalog of criminal behaviors whose essence in turn fuels Her need for domination. And it's Her smell that casts dominion.

I pull my T-shirt tight, forming a snug noose around my neck. A tourniquet which I twist just enough to cut off my breath. To thicken the pulse, causing dizziness. A dream state of asphyxia is where I find Her. Lurking in the corner of my impending death. A bewitching pariah summoned only when everything else has been blotted out, chased away, erased, when nothing else remains but Her. And the mind is free to roam the inner recess of my imagination. The imagination She stained with Her scent. The images saturated with Her effervescence. The fantasies and recollections with which I shall remain forever trapped . . .

A downtown alley in the back of a theater once glorious, now in ruins . . . a sleazy European soft-porn skin flick milks what little life is left in the six or seven scummy patrons who scrounged up the two dollars and fifty cent admission fee. The cheesy soundtrack of '70s synth is offset by overdubs whose grunts and groans simulate real passion. It bleeds through the brick. I'm leaning against the wall slippery with greasy rain. Her right hand is cocked around my throat. Her left unbuckles my jeans. She pulls me out, half hard, shiny with heat. I can smell myself. She begins squeezing. Tugging. Jerking. Whispering, I'll suck you until you cry like a little girl . . . *I pull Her into me, my lips touch Her neck. The pungent musk, my eventual downfall . . . She shoves my hands away, slaps my mouth, insists I do not move.* Stay still. Don't speak. Don't breathe. *I hold my breath.*

She slides down my body into a squat, legs spread wide, exposing her pink. Tells me to not even dream of peeking. I'm not allowed to look. Insists I turn my head left, no right, to keep an eye on the entrance to the alley. To keep a look out, make sure no porn patrons decide they need a piss, no cops come nosing around, no teenagers or gangbangers. No dogs or dopers.

She puts me in her mouth. Her soft fat lips encircle the purple tip. Nip on it. Bite it. A little too hard. Enough to make me wince. Nestling teeth inside the foreskin. She coos on it making sarcastic sucking sounds, loud enough to startle. Then swallows. The whole of my cock. Lips flush to pubis. I fear She will somehow disgorge the meat from my body. Suck it off. Spit it out. Step on it. She holds my cock undulating in her throat.

Squeezing. Forcing me to spasm, flinch, thrash. Come. Her mouth slowly subsides, leaving me limp. She slaps at my prick, insisting I put it away . . . get it out of Her face, that filthy thing, a discarded toy no longer of interest. I scramble to stuff it back inside my pants. My belt buckle chimes against the brick wall. The jingle of silver and stone is transformed into wood against steel.

My daydream fades as Holtzer and O'Leary begin their afternoon shift. Rattling the cages with nightsticks. With bullshit and intimidation. Dirty jokes and catcalls. The stink of their aftershave. Body count begins. I don't know why they bother. No one has ever mastered a successful break. The last man who tried was riddled with fifty-two bullets. Back in '73, or so I've heard. I've only been inside for six months, twelve days, seven hours, and forty-one minutes. I'll be released in twenty-four some-odd years. If I can make it. I can't believe I have for this long. Don't know how anyone does. Surprised the suicide rate isn't higher. That there's not more manslaughter. Homicide's not on the rise. The smell alone makes you pray for murder, for only in death will there be the freedom of relief, that portal of escape from which release will breathe new air. An air devoid of ghosted scents whose putrefaction stains the brain stem.

Second only to the smells are the sounds. The moronic chattering, nonstop bantering, petty squabbles, chronic bickering, inflated bragging. The ceaseless tedium of being forced to endure countless conversations full of run-on sentences whose main objective is to overflow every second with a hideous din which murders silence . . . The cruelest of all punishments . . . The caterwauling of stupid men in love with the sound of their own voices . . . The endless boredom and monotonous routine occasionally eclipsed by the static sounds of shitty reruns sputtering from a broken-down black-and-white TV propped at the far end of the corridor, featuring only the finest in adult entertainment—

AMERICA'S MOST WANTED, HOLLYWOOD CONFIDENTIAL, THE PEOPLE'S COURT, TEXAS JUSTICE, LAW & ORDER: SPECIAL VICTIMS UNIT, CSI: LAS VEGAS/MIAMI/NEW YORK, EXTREME EVIDENCE, FORENSIC FILES, PSYCHIC DETECTIVES, COPS, AMERICAN JUSTICE . . . Now that's ripe.

I am surrounded by petty hustlers, two-bit thieves, pathological liars, serial killers, and pedophiles all obsessed with the crimes of their brothers. Surrounded by men who have murdered their wives, stalked their girlfriends, killed their boyfriends, kidnapped the kids who should have been aborted. Hardcore criminals who gleam a perverse solace in the nightly repetition of slick reenactments of crimes so complex it takes a team of half a dozen well-paid television writers to concoct the plot.

Still, no distraction is ever great enough to allow you to forget where you are, what you did, what went wrong. How easily a stupid mistake—which could have been avoided, should never have happened, was not intended and was not my fault, for which I am forever fucked—can ruin your life.

* * *

We never went to Her place. She never even mentioned it. Not in the three weeks that I knew Her. I don't even know if She had one. She couldn't stand to have sex in enclosed spaces. She said it made Her feel trapped, domesticated. Depressed. It was boring. Dull. Too damn rote. It always had to be outside, in plain sight, in public view. The threat of being caught, possibly arrested for indecent exposure, turned Her on. Made Her rabid. She claimed it was one of Her many personal attacks against the ridiculous and outdated regulations fostered on society by Government Issue. Viewed public indecency, lewd behavior, and exhibitionism as a personal vendetta against the abolition of the individual. If we lived in a truly free society, pleasure would be rewarded, not punished . . .

I know, I know, I should have known better . . .

A Korean late-night mini-mart. We went in for cigarettes, two cups of rank coffee, something sweet. Last aisle near the frozen food. Between the baby diapers and the dish-washing detergent. We were babbling like schoolkids, giggling like idiots. Spewing convoluted utopian rhetoric like college freshmen. She pulled me close. Stuck Her tongue in my mouth. Started sucking it. Instant arousal. And my hand between Her legs. Petting sweetly. "Pinch it," She insisted. Biting my lower lip, Her eyes trained on the mirror above us, the view it afforded the cashier. Making Her twitch. Wiggle. She unbuttoned my shirt, eyes glued to our reflection. Began sucking my nipples. Licking them, slurping loudly. Her slippery little tongue, a rattler, darting back and forth across my chest. Chewing, a hungry little orphan eating a gumdrop.

The small things are what you miss most. The inconsequential. A warm breeze on the back of your neck. A fresh pack of cigarettes. The smell of wet leaves. Mud. Music. The Sunday paper. Silence. Try keeping your mouth shut when Holtzer, impeccable in his freshly starched uniform, lightning-bolt tattoos barely concealed under his black armband, poster boy for the Aryan Brotherhood, makes his afternoon rounds . . . interrupts my reverie . . . I could almost scream at the bastard to just back off, shut the fuck up, drop dead.

Big man. Bigger mouth. Feels it his duty to comment on every guy in the ward. "Make up that bunk!" "You pussies look a little pallid today . . . What's the matter, meatloaf no good?" "Another beautiful day in paradise." "Greet the day, you low-life shits!" Thinks it improves morale, his useless drivel. Please . . . Pretends to befriend all the white cons. I get his trip. Sieg heil and all that bullshit. I try to keep to myself. Toe the line. Not talk. An almost Zen existence where days, weeks, and soon years will disappear in meditation, daydreams. Memories.

A light rain . . . quarter past midnight, bus stop. Downtown. All but deserted. Only the truly desperate out on a night like this. A wino or two drenched in cardboard, stooped down low in the corner of a faraway building . . . A crack whore waiting to roll an unsuspecting mark, the rustling of tin cans as they scamper up the sidewalk. I'm with Her again . . . She straddles me on the bench. Climbs over my lap.

Long black raincoat, short black dress. Not a word is spoken. She's devouring my face. Biting cheeks, forehead, ears, neck. I thrash my head from side to side, trying to avoid those pointy incisors. A manic dingo, ferocious, feral. She keeps up the attack. It's all I can stand. I stuff a musty leather glove in Her mouth, damp from rain, smelling of cigarettes and mildew. She clamps down, glowering. Not much time before Her next attack.

I grab Her hands behind Her back, holding Her small wrists in one meaty fist. Hard. I tweak them a little. Until I hear Her gasp. Quiver. I rip Her panties aside.

I want to hurt Her as She hurt me, my face still throbbing full of love bites from this petite piranha. She struggles against the force, pinned in place, but there's nowhere for Her to turn. The other musty glove grabs at Her pouty puss. Her musky smell mingles with the stench of wet streets ringed with garbage. Inflames me beyond belief. I stuff my fingers inside, two at a time, poking viciously at Her tender pink.

Now She's the one who thrashes. Left and right, a slow gurgle of excitement slips past Her mushy gag. Both mouths now stuffed with the stink of moldy leather. I force another finger inside and then another. All but my thumb. Which rests against Her swell, that niblet of pleasure. Mashed against the pressure. Causing Her to buck, a wild little bitch, sent into heat. I begin a steady pummel. Punching at that little hole, pounding, forcing a grand expansion, explosion, expulsion. She comes spraying all over the glove, my coat and jeans, the bench.

An abstract portrait rendered in spunk.

She set me up. But I was stupid enough to take the fall. She slipped into my life like a low-grade fever. A bacterial infection, which quickly poisons every reasonable cell in the body until you're defenseless against the virulent blows of Her night sickness. My whole being tainted by Her toxic succulence, a psychic pollution so potent that the only recourse was acquiescence as She leeched at my life force. Devouring small pieces of myself which fell away like dust, dry bones, dead skin, desert wind.

Now time keeps me. With slow dissolve every hour dribbles away, every second stretched to eternity, the

minutes mere interludes with which I count my heart-
beats. Leaking life from my caged existence like sand
in an endless hourglass whose bottomless pit mocks
without mercy . . . stealing from me the most precious
commodity. The choice to decide just how I'll waste the
day. Do not take this lightly. It is the finest of luxuries.
Now my days are wasted for me. Locked up and lost in
thoughts whose instant replay is my only salvation.

I calibrate time by plucking hairs. Off my arms, my
legs, my pubis, and my eyebrows. Glued to the four-
by-eight-by-nine-foot walls with spittle. Prehistoric as
a miniature cave painting. My private museum. Filled
floor to ceiling with masterpieces I create in invisible ink,
sketched by fingernail into the canvas of my flesh. Projected through the filter of my brainpan onto the gallery
walls whose seething funk I erase with my gluey iris and
replace with much eye strain and a headache-inducing
squint with pristine white plasterboard filled with a
nonstop rotating film loop replicating Rubens, Brueghel,
Bosch, Bellini, Bernini, Goya, Caravaggio.

The Masters whose subjects not unlike myself were
forced by circumstances beyond their control into
playing victim at the hands of cruel gods and vicious
monsters whose only offering of salvation beyond this
tortured existence was in the knowledge that a suffering that wounds beyond the shallow exterior of flesh
and bone—penetrating through the multiple levels of
epidermis into and beyond every fiber of your being, an
agony from which no solitary moment without would
ever again be complete—is offered up in loving submission to a greater being. A being with no equal. Whose
godlike powers and omnipotent understanding, no mat-

ter how cruelly projected, or simultaneously you are re-
jected from it, is reward unto itself. A being who in my
case has disappeared completely from my life, appearing
only in visions as apparition and savior.

PART IV

ROUGHNECKS

HUBERT SELBY JR.

THE MAN WHO REFUSED TO DIE

Born in 1928 in the Badlands of Brooklyn, Hubert Selby Jr. stomped a new asshole in the face of literature with his first novel *Last Exit to Brooklyn*. Published in 1964 and committed to film in 1990, it remains one of the most harrowing and influential works of American literature. With each consecutive masterpiece—*The Room, The Demon, Requiem for a Dream, Song of the Silent Snow,* and *The Willow Tree*—Selby forced his readers into emotional battlecades where obsession, violence, and madness colored the scars bearing witness to lessons learned the hard way. He died in April 2004 from chronic lung disease.

This interview was conducted under interrogation lights in Selby's Los Angeles bachelor pad in 2001.

LL: Your books have inspired the last three generations of writers, myself included . . . Did writing save your life?

HS: I don't doubt it, in probably more than one way. The basic thing was it gave me a purpose. It gave me a reason to bother living . . . I started writing because I wanted to do something with my life before I died. Because I kept dying. It became a way of life. I think that was the most important thing. Everybody needs some reason to live. There may not be a reason for this life, but we all need a reason to live. It has a very therapeutic value to it . . . If I wouldn't have written, I might have exploded, who the hell knows . . .

LL: Writing as release valve . . . Blow off steam in the pressure cooker . . . When and why did you leave New York?

HS: 1965 . . . there was a job offer. In retrospect, I was just trying to get away from *me* . . . I was just out of my head . . . in all kinds of trouble, so I came out here, but of course I brought me with me. I always do. I can't seem to leave me behind . . . So I stayed in California till '78, went back east till '83, and I've been here since then.

LL: Do you miss it?

HS: Very, very much . . . You're born and raised in a city, then you live in a place like L.A., it's not even a suburb . . . it's just a big nothing. But the New York that I miss doesn't exist anymore. Physically it's gone, plus the people—that's what really makes the memories—are now all over the place, if they're still alive. One day I just decided I would enjoy this town for what it has instead of bitching about what it hasn't.

LL: There's a real dynamic between the East and West Coast. A definite East Coast snobbery. The basis of our reality is so different. It doesn't get much more real than withstanding the battlefields of Brooklyn, especially coming up as you did in the 1930s and '40s . . . You enlisted in the Merchant Marines—why?

HS: It only lasted a couple of years before I got sick. I always wanted to go to sea, there was a war going on, and it became easy for people to lie about their age. Who knows how many millions of kids did . . . I was fifteen when I first started in the New York City Harbor. At sixteen I started sailing to Europe. That was 1945-6. In September of 1946 I got pulled off the ship, they said I was going to die.

LL: Most people who caught TB at that time didn't survive.

HS: The stress of the war, the hygiene conditions, lack of nutrition . . . I was in the hospital for about four years. I had ten ribs cut out, the whole story . . .

LL: Did you read a lot?

HS: That's when I started reading. Mickey Spillane, all the shoot-'em-ups. You could read a couple a day.

LL: Was *The Room* inspired by time actually spent incarcerated?

HS: Yeah . . .

LL: So, if you weren't tortured enough by having TB, multiple operations, and being incarcerated in a hospital for four years . . .

HS: Well, I didn't realize it at the time, but I became institutionalized . . . Any time the world became too much, I could always end up in an institution. The great thing about institutions is that you can bitch and moan and everybody agrees with you. *Yeah, we've all been screwed* . . . There's no responsibilities. You don't have to worry about anything. Except it interferes with your freedom.

LL: Drug bust?

HS: I got busted in September of '67 for heroin. Boiled down to possession or driving under the influence. Out here in L.A.

LL: How hard was it to get *Last Exit to Brooklyn* published?

HS: One night I was down at the Cedar Tavern, where we all used to hang out and Amiri Baraka [poet, political activist] suggested I try Sterling Lord, who was Jack Kerouac's agent. I sent them a manuscript, they called me back and said, *I think we can make money here.* He gave it to Barney Rosset at Grove Press, who at that time was probably one of the greatest publishers in the country, and they published it.

LL: What was your advance?

HS: I think maybe a few hundred bucks . . .

LL: Did you hang out with the Beats?

HS: No.

LL: Did they interest you?

HS: Not really . . . I read one or two of Jack's books.

LL: You're occasionally painted into the same corner as the Beats. What's the difference between you and them?

HS: When they talk about the Beats, they're talking about forty or fifty different writers. What I disagree with is the people who called themselves Beatniks had the idea that if they just put words on paper, it was good. No technique, no discipline, no craft, no art. Just "*I did it.*" If you picked up an instrument and tooted or threw paint on something, then that's Art. I just don't believe that.

LL: *The Willow Tree* . . . Last time we spoke you referred to it as a sixteen-year incubation . . . Relief at last? The longest pregnancy on record?

HS: I don't know about that, but I can sure look an elephant in the eye with that one. It was very difficult. The end of something and the beginning of something else. I had to break through somehow. I had the book clearly in mind since 1983. But when I actually started writing, I'd write for a few weeks, then one day I'd get up to go inside and write and I'd get close to the door, but something would just pick me up and throw me out of the room. Sometimes I'd have to try for a few weeks just to get in the room. The actual writing took maybe six months, but it happened over a period of many years. Each time I did get back to work, I had to write my way back into the rhythm of the book because there might be six months to a year between writing sessions. It was originally 700 pages. I had to cut out about 300 pages. It was a strange, painful experience. The most painful book to write.

LL: The main theme of *The Willow Tree* is that in the face of desperation and violence, one man who has overcome the nightmare of his life and has survived is trying with all his strength to not relinquish hope. Was it difficult as a writer who concentrates on the darker side of life to detail redemptive themes in a way you as a reader can respect?

HS: The actual writing was not the problem . . .

LL: Just the ghost in the doorway . . . ?

HS: It might be as simple and obvious as my past had me by the fruits and didn't want me to do this, didn't want my freedom. It tried to prevent me from breaking loose from the past.

LL: When were you the happiest?

HS: Before I was born . . .

LL: In the womb?

HS: No, no . . . that was horrible . . . That's when I started to die . . .

LL: Torture begins in the womb.

HS: That's right, man! I started to die thirty-six hours before I was born. By the time I was born, it was hopeless, I was blue from cyanosis, I had a couple kinds of brain damage, my head was out of shape, it was just extraordinary . . . My mother had toxemia, she didn't know what to do about breast feeding, the doctor said, *Don't worry, he'll eventually suck out all the poison* . . . So that's how I started life . . . pissed off . . .

LL: THE MAN WHO REFUSED TO DIE . . . Are you a dirty old man?

HS: Am I old? I guess I am . . . I'm seventy-one . . . I was born a dirty old man.

Bibliography: Hubert Selby Jr.

Last Exit to Brooklyn (1964)
The Room (1971)
The Demon (1976)
Requiem for a Dream (1978)
Song of the Silent Snow (1986)
The Willow Tree (1998)
Waiting Period (2002)

NICK TOSCHES

SQUALOR AND SPLENDOR

Introduction by Mike Ryan
Interview by Lydia Lunch, 2002

Rhythm and structure. Very simple concepts that provide the basis for poetry. The foundations of epic works by the likes of Homer and Dante. Through simple components these authors addressed the major themes of life, all of which drive toward the same infernal question: Why do I exist?

In the Gospel of Thomas, Nick Tosches found a simple rule, as basic and obvious as the most elementary algebraic equation and as powerful as nuclear fusion: "If you bring forth what is within you, what you bring forth will save you. If you do not bring forth what is within you, what you do not bring forth will destroy you."

But first he would steal books. And find other simple aphorisms: "Death to the living, long life to the killers." Became a barroom porter at fourteen. Worked and then abandoned a stint as a paste-up artist for the Lovable Underwear Company. Snake-hunted in Florida. And then a conclusion: "Immature writers plagiarize, mature writers steal."

Tosches became a music critic in New York City for *Creem* magazine in the 1970s alongside cohorts Lester

Bangs and Richard Meltzer. While he was living in the neighborhood of the burgeoning punk/new wave culture and interviewing people like Patti Smith and Blondie, his tendencies led him toward old country-music outlaws and other originators of rock and roll. After his years at *Creem*, he began his work as a biographer, the vast majority of which focused on men caught in the grips of good and evil. Musician Jerry Lee Lewis. Boxer Sonny Liston. Mob boss Michele Sindona.

Through his novels, a screenplay, poetry, and his own commentary, it is apparent that Tosches himself has also struggled with good and evil, darkness and light, and the insanity which accompanies these things. But while he pursues the high calling of wrestling demons, he also engages in the elusive thing called solitude, sometimes known as the art of doing nothing. That which Nick Tosches cares about above all things is the feral desire to live, in a world where survival depends on cash flow. Hence the introductory quote to *The Nick Tosches Reader*:

> "Now, Mr. Faulkner," she said, "what were you thinking of when you wrote that?"
> "Money," he replied.

In the year 2000, Tosches released the tiniest of books called *The Last Opium Den*. It chronicles his quest to find not only pure opium as a treatment for his recently diagnosed diabetic condition, but also to satisfy his romantic desire to experience an opium den itself. The book opens with the line, *You see, I needed to go to Hell. I was, you might say, homesick*. A tour through the Asian underworld eventually leads him to a shack somewhere in

Indochina. The romantic vision of the opium den proves untenable, but he makes do and reposes for an indefinite period of time savoring "God's own medicine."

That place which he had left, run by "these rubes who turned New York into a PG-rated mall and who oh so loved it thus," would beckon him. Nick Tosches finally returned to a New York City filled with ghosts, to deliver his own blood, and he has been restless ever since.

LL: I have to say that I hate the impersonal nature of phone interviews. I prefer to actually smell my subjects. I thought that maybe we could just set the stage a little.

NT: Okay.

LL: It is 7:45 a.m. I am in L.A. I am sitting near a window. It is still wet with night-blooming jasmine. I am wearing a thin black slip. I'm barefoot. I got hair in my eyes and I'm smoking a Lucky Strike and drinking a Cuban coffee. What about you?

NT: Okay. I've been . . . awake . . . since yesterday morning because I've been up all night writing this wretched garbage, or trying to write it. I already had to go out at 6 in the morning to get stuff notarized, then FedEx it. And now I'm sitting here. I got nothin' on but this old robe. There's a plumber here fixing the toilet bowl. It's hot, but I've opened the windows, and I got the fan on. I'm smoking . . . a Camel . . . through a Dunhill cigarette holder, and I'm drinking what they call . . . I think it's Vienna Sumatra coffee. And off in the distance is the plumber.

LL: I was up until about 7 a.m. I fell asleep about ten

minutes before I was supposed to call you. I was up all night too, so we're in the same shape. You still live in New York City?

NT: I still do. I wish I only lived here part of the time. I get out of the country a lot, but I still want to have a place out of the country, and I don't. So yeah, I live in New York.

LL: I put in a decade in New York City. Every step I take there, I feel like I'm crushing ghosts.

NT: Oh yeah, well . . .

LL: Do you think New York still possesses the same manic electricity that has stimulated so much great art?

NT: No. That's a good way to put it, with the ghosts. The New York that I love has completely vanished. So I'm living in a limbo with an umbilical cord . . . to nowhere.

LL: You said you leave the country a lot. Where to?

NT: I was going to Paris a lot, because I had this girlfriend there. She dumped me, or I dumped her, or something. I spent a lot of time in Sicily. But now I just have to stay here and do this work because it's all a year overdue.

LL: What is a year overdue?

NT: Garbage. Complete, wretched, DRECK. I have to do two magazine stories, and then a book, and it's all wretched dreck and I just need to work my way out to freedom. If I had the money I would just give everybody their money back and not do any of it. It's too much.

LL: But you're chained to it for now.

NT: That's it, yeah! I'm just resigned to it and my only consolation is I am not going to sign any more contracts or take any more money from anybody once this is all completely cleared up. Freedom. That's all I want.

LL: You just finished *In the Hand of Dante*?

NT: Yes—it takes place during the last year of Dante's life, and simultaneously right now, in the present. It's about how the most beatific spiritual vision can become a force of great evil.

LL: That's a subject you are often drawn to, men who are being torn apart by the battle of good and evil.

NT: Or the ambiguity of what's good and what's evil. And who invented what first.

LL: Territory you covered in your books on Jerry Lee Lewis, Sonny Liston, and the book *Trinities*.

NT: Yeah.

LL: Writers, by their very nature, are vain, narcissistic . . . We spend most of our days alone. How much do you struggle in your own life with assholism, with cruelty, with intolerance? And is that what you're trying to understand better by tackling these subjects?

NT: I don't know if I'm trying to understand it. I'm all right with just turning away from everything at this point. I know that *In the Hand of Dante* has really upset . . . and even revolted a lot of people. On the other hand, it's been called a work of great beauty. In Italy and Germany they're just terrified of it.

LL: It's interesting how different countries interpret things.

NT: Yeah! But at this point, I am basically ready to pack it in. I want seven years of absolute nothingness. A seven-year stretch, before I croak. Next year is as good a time as any to start it.

LL: Well, writing dominates your entire life when you're working on something.

NT: Yeah, well, I hate it!

LL: It dominates everything. And back to the methodology, what is your procedure?

NT: Of working?

LL: Are you in lockdown?

NT: Yeah! Although I could spend hours working, writing something I love, whether it's an essay about something that nobody's ever gonna give me a dime for, or a poem, or some obscure animal of a wisp of a notion or a line. There's always this wretched stuff where I know I must perform within the perimeters of a given stage. I just can't seem to do it until my back is against the wall. Until everything is overloading me to the point of impossibility. And so, thus . . . okay! See . . . I spend enormous sums of money. My idea of fleeing involves money. But there's no money. It becomes like the snake that bites its own tail. That's it. But I can't fulfill these commitments. And they always involve people who wanna pay me the most, yet never want what I can do best.

LL: So what you love turns into what you hate.

NT: It's almost like, *So why do you want ME to do it?* Yeah, I do hate it. And then there's this diseased aspect of my mind where as much as I hate it, I'll get so involved in it, and go off into such obsessive detail rather than just go in there and be a hack. That's all I really need to do to do the job properly. I don't even seem to be capable of that! It's like the travails of boredom.

LL: You said you need a seven-year break, which is understandable. You've been incredibly prolific.

NT: I want a seven-year stretch of nothingness.

LL: Shoot the clock.

NT: Yeah.

LL: Start there. I've read you frequent the same restaurant every day for lunch. Do you employ other regimens to free up more of your time to just write?

NT: I'll tell you the truth. Until the other day, I hadn't written anything since last year. That's how bad this situation really is. It's a joke. I have these two articles that are a year . . . more than a year overdue. I've just begun one of them, and the guy who's waiting for this garbage book from HarperCollins keeps calling my agent and saying, *How's the book coming?* The book is now at the end of the list! He's looking at next year, at best. Now I want to get everything out of the way by . . . let's say . . . when the first warm breeze of next year blows.

LL: How did you first come into contact with Hubert Selby?

NT: The first time . . . oh Jesus! I first came into contact with him twenty years ago, when he was living in New York. I was at my blackest, most chilling, deadliest period. It was right around when I finished *Trinities.* Everybody was telling me I was gonna die. I asked Selby's publisher where he was. I figured, if *he* was still alive, that means I could fuckin' live forever. I wrote him a letter. He basically turned out saving my life, for the time being. I was really reaching out for darkness, and I got light instead. We built a new friendship over the last six or seven years. Time flies when you don't work.

LL: What were you doing that was so death defying?

NT: I was just being what I was. Which was doing exactly what I wanted to do. Which was being in a state of oblivion for months at a time, only interrupting it to get dragged off to the hospital.

LL: Was it alcohol, or anything you could get your hands on?

NT: It was alcohol and everything else. It was mostly unbelievably huge sums of alcohol, and then I would, on top of that, go for heroin, or whatever. It was electricity from booze that was keeping me alive. I didn't see any other way to be, or one single valid reason for me to be any different.

LL: Selby's so inspirational. That he's managed to live in this fragile body with so much energy!

NT: I know! He's Johnny No-Lungs, ya know?

LL: When I started doing spoken word, and realized that he was still alive, I contacted him. And at that point he hadn't been doing many shows. I was just amazed that the guy was interested, wanted to do it, and had the stamina.

NT: Though he'll never see it as such, I think he did, if not literally save my life, at least take me and head me toward some piercing wisdom. There was one thing he said to me, one line. He said, *Never look for light to enter you. Try to find the light that's been buried and let it out.* It was like the Gospel of Thomas. I do things my own way. And I'd gone so long without drinking, I realized that I could never drink hard liquor again. Because I knew it would take over my body and my soul. Physically it would. So I said, *Let me try to drink a beer.* And I found out that I could go out and drink beer, and not drink the next morning. Then I lost my taste for beer, and I became an expensive wino, who just relaxes with it.

LL: You quoted the Gospel of Thomas. Did Selby turn you on to that?

NT: No, no! I found that one on my own. It was almost exactly what he was saying, though. Whether he was aware of it or not, there was such a parallel. But he brought it home so piercingly, because of how he said it. He's a treasure and this country should be placing laurel leaves on his head, and gold bars at his feet. They're not doing it.

LL: They'll wait till he dies, and he'll still be lucky to get the recognition he deserves then.

NT: Writers are the only people that get paid posthumously. Selby will be fucking rich twelve years after he's dead, after it becomes required buying.

LL: Do you still drink?

NT: Yeah. I drink two glasses of wine a day with lunch. To me, lunch is the highlight of my existence. Like I said, my New York doesn't exist anymore. I don't go out. There's nowhere for me to go and see old friends. Or to even walk down blocks that are pleasant. The social clubs I used to go to are now like some kind of chi-chi shoe store or something, Korean dry cleaners . . . so it's all gone now and lunch is the time for me to relax, a few glasses. And now, maybe once a month or so, I'll purposely go out to drink too much. The thing is, I've turned into an expensive wino so I only drink good wine. I don't drink at home. So if I go out I have to bring my own wine with me. That's my routine now. Yesterday I didn't drink anything, I didn't leave the house. I worked. I looked at the clock and it was 10 o'clock, and then it was 10 o'clock at night, and then it was 2 o'clock, and I figured, well, I'll just keep going. And here I am.

LL: You mentioned before your flamboyance, that you like to spend extravagant—

NT: —amounts of money, yeah.

LL: Is that a rebellion, or—

NT: Nah. It's just that I never had anything when I was young and once I got a taste of it, I figured, *Well, this is what the money's for?* I try to share it, and lavish it on myself. I figure that that's just what it was for.

LL: You've gotta spoil yourself.

NT: Yeah, and . . . that's it.

LL: I'm gonna quote you, from *The Last Opium Den*: "Enough of this profundity. The labor involved in its elucidation is far too great. You want enlightenment? Go get it yourself . . . paradise has no words." That's so beautiful. What do you know at fifty—are you fifty now?

NT: I'm more than fifty.

LL: What do you know at fifty something that you wouldn't have admitted to yourself at twenty-five?

NT: Oh, well . . . at twenty-five I never, ever, ever would have perceived of the value and the power of just being completely, openly honest. I would have been both afraid of it and also would think of it as being destructive to something. Now I realize that it's just the only fuckin' way. I also know now that I have a very palpable sense of life being finite, and therefore being less willing to sacrifice any of it to bullshit. I'm more aware of the main events, which is that every single breath, this very breath now, is really the only gift that we have. Without that, there's nothing. It's the most immense gift. That's a beautiful, beautiful thing. Also, I don't have to put up with anything I don't want to put up with. Fuck 'em. If it weren't for the fact that I can't stand the idea of being in jail, I would just go around shootin' people. Just to shut 'em up, you know.

LL: The problem with that thought, and I entertain it daily . . . I just don't have enough fuckin' bullets.

NT: Just hearing myself say it, it reinforces how much I believe that. I'm glad that you somehow got me to articulate it. At this very moment while I feel half dead. Now I got half a smile on my weary face. I'm just gonna jump in the shower and . . . I think . . . go have my lunch. Then come back and collapse.

Bibliography: Nick Tosches
Country: The Twisted Roots of Rock 'n' Roll (1977)
Hellfire: The Jerry Lee Lewis Story (1982)
Unsung Heroes of Rock 'n' Roll: The Birth of Rock in the Wild Years before Elvis (1984)
Power on Earth (1986)
Cut Numbers (1988)
Dino: Living High in the Dirty Business of Dreams (1992)
Trinities (1994)
Chaldea and I Dig Girls (1999)
The Devil and Sonny Liston (2000)
The Nick Tosches Reader (2000)
Where Dead Voices Gather (2001)
In the Hand of Dante (2002)
The Last Opium Den (2002)
King of the Jews: The Greatest Mob Story Never Told (2005)

JERRY STAHL

THE LIVING PERV

Jerry Stahl restores my faith in contemporary writing. His memoir *Permanent Midnight* detailed one of the most harrowing and hilarious journeys into degeneracy and drug addiction ever published. Stahl followed it with *Perv—A Love Story*, a belly-slapping good time (at the expense of his own manhood) chronicling cringe-inducing pubescent sexual scenarios involving failed, fractured, and just plain fucked-up romantic encounters. *Plain Clothes Naked* comes on its heels, a fat contemporary detective noir whose punch line features a purloined polaroid of George W.'s nutsack. Brilliant.

In June of 1999 I had the pleasure of strapping Stahl to a plush red-velvet sofa in my living room for forty-five minutes of psychotherapy that left us both spent, soaked in sweat, convulsing in fever, and delirious with the opportunity to once more stroke each other's ego in a verbal tongue-to-brain fuck.

LL: After *Permanent Midnight*, did you feel you had more to live up to or more to live down? It was a huge revelation dealing with the worst low points in your own personal life.

JS: Neither. Just putting it out there in a way that seemed deeply remarkable and disturbo at the time, but as soon as you do it seems completely pedestrian. So all the shit that is shocking to Joe Square is Mickey Mouse to a whole other population. I don't think it's about living it up or down, it's about finding another disgusting quarry to mine.

LL: What do you think failed about the film version?

JS: I don't think it failed. I think it succeeded in what it was trying to do. I thought the acting was great, it was just a different kind of asshole than what's painted in the book. Once you take the money, I think you've just got to shut the fuck up.

LL: The many sides to our assholism . . . Was it horrifying to know that your life was projected not only up on the big screen, but eventually would be invading other people's homes via cable TV?

JS: The horrifying thing is, is that it wasn't my life, it was somebody else's version of my life. So it was a relief that Jon Bon Jovi wasn't playing me and they didn't change the drug to ecstasy. There's no muscle, gland, or corner of the brain that's been evolved to deal with the fact that people are going to be staring at you over their bunions in their bed, at some really off portrayal of you. It's so disturbing and so weird that I don't even think about it . . . It's somewhere between denial and oblivion.

LL: No matter how much we reveal in our writing and readings, I find the most satisfaction in gloating over the things people *don't* know . . . Do you feel the same? You're exposing more in one book than most people have to deal with in their entire lifetime

JS: I'm exposing what seems like the truth at the time. I couldn't write *Permanent Midnight* now. Everything is completely different. I was ten minutes clean. My nerve ends were completely flapping in the wind.

LL: Do you think writing was a huge part of your recovery?

JS: Who the fuck knows? It got me out of the bathroom down the hall from the queens-next-door nightmare I was living in on Sunset Boulevard. When I didn't have a place of my own. On the corner of Crack and Eightball . . . taking a shit at Musso & Frank's because I didn't have a toilet. It got me out of there.

LL: Did sex change a lot after you got clean?

JS: Absolutely.

LL: Better or worse?

JS: If you'd never fucked anyone without being totally loaded, it's really terrifying. There's no place to hide. So on one level it's terrifically hot because you're feeling everything. On the other hand, it's paralyzingly disturbing because you can't chemically stage set the experience. I had to fuck people for money, shelter, food, drugs. I was a chemically altered whore in a lot of ways. Then I stopped being a whore, stopped being chemically altered, and I wasn't sure what the fuck was underneath it. If anything. The no-place-to-hide-ness of it is probably spectacularly healthy for that reason.

LL: What's so amazing, especially about your readings and the details in *Perv*, is that most men spend their entire lives bragging about the sexual prowess they will never possess, yet you willingly expose some of the most excruciating and humiliating sexual experiences of your life. You must be a sexual master.

JS: I wonder if shame has become my new heroin. It really

is embarrassing in one way, but at the same time you get strung out on revelation. On saying the unsayable. I'm sure you know that. It's another kind of drug. I had a woman come up to me and say, *I can't believe you said your penis at rest was the size of . . .* What did I say?

LL: An acorn.

JS: An acorn at rest. And she said the same thing: *You must be really confident.*

LL: Has it made it easier to score with women? Are they lining up to throw down?

JS: I said, *Let's focus on the phrase "at rest."* It's the accordion factor. Let's march that out right now. As a wise woman once said, *Jerry, you have nothing to be ashamed of . . . You're a hard average.* I was so proud at that moment. At fifteen or sixteen, that's how it is. The reason it was so fresh to me is because there's a cliché about recovery from dope or whatever substance, and it's true. You stop developing emotionally at the age you start using every day. Okay, so I wash ashore clean and I may be in my forties, but in my head I'm feeling what guys are feeling at fourteen. Which is a weird vulnerability. When you stay hard on a speedball for seven hours, your standards are a little warped back in the real world. At my age, you'll blow your prostate out your fucking ear.

LL: Especially if the person you're screwing isn't on the same chemical high.

JS: I was always with straight women. But the only women I ever actually had relationships with were ex-hookers, ex–dope fiends, horrifying survivors of God knows what kind of abuse, because they're the

only people who, in my state of exposed nerve end-
ings, I can actually be with. I fall in love with their
pain, they fall in love with mine. And that's where
the sex comes from.

LL: Pain is the great divide. Those who have walked
barefoot into the mouth of the volcano and those
who haven't. And if you haven't, you're just not on
the same level of understanding.

JS: That brings it back to something you asked before
about revealing all this. I'm the luckiest motherfucker
in the world. Because having done that, I don't need
to hide. Anybody that can relate to me will, anybody
who doesn't isn't in my face. The groupies I would
get, the one-in-a-hundred women who would actually want to be locked in an elevator with me are so
bent anyway that I can fucking relax.

Bibliography: Jerry Stahl
Permanent Midnight: A Memoir (1995)
Perv—A Love Story (1999)
Plainclothes Naked (2001)
I, Fatty: A Novel (2004)
Love Without: Stories (2007)
Pain Killers (2009)

THE VIOLENT DISBELIEF
OF RON ATHEY

If the inside of your head gets pummeled with enough emotional blunt-force trauma to splinter the psyche, you develop ways to punish the body, that fleshy prison which houses the pain.

When the agony of life's relentless frustration is steeped in the malignant tyranny of deception and abuse, and the ones closest to you deny not only their culpability, but worship at the feet of false idols to justify the perpetuation of their violence, your trusty friend the razor will never tell a single lie.

If the sight of blood brought forth from your own hand spells an almost immediate relief, a sublime release of pressure, consider yourself a member in an elite coven who strive to decode the mystery of self-sacrifice. Whereby a violation you now control can provide a temporary satiation, a stifling of the nauseating screams and endless insinuations of a world turned inside out.

The undeniable aroma of skin melting under the cigarette's ugly kiss localizes the all-consuming daily irritants until it fills yellow with pus, leaks out, drains, scabs over, and is eventually picked clean, revealing a fresh growth of virgin pink. As the wounds heal and the blistered skin renews with life, these marks of identity play as time capsule which can further separate you from the original sinner, the antagonist responsible for your infection, a soul sickness born of pain and loss.

The cycle of abuse changes course only once you have decided to own your self-flagellation. Not simply as revenge or repetition of the crimes committed against you, but in celebration as ritual to all that has been willfully overcome.

This is the first commandment of the new testament in accordance with the Bible of Pope Ron Athey.

Throughout the 1990s, Athey's Torture Trilogy was both a pageant to and a lurid slur against classic religious imagery and its relationship to the eternal themes of death and disease. The 1991 production of *Martyrs and Saints* illustrated the cruel and impersonal nature of supposed "caregivers." Three nurses, lips sutured closed, lead three mummified bodies on gurneys into the operating theater where the bodies are violated with enemas, specula, and genital piercing.

1994's *Four Scenes in a Harsh Life* opens with an androgynous St. Sebastian pierced with arrows and covered with oil. Athey acting as Holy Woman proceeds to anoint the audience with the saint's greasy runoff. The second act, entitled "Steakhouse Motherfuckers," is a twisted pantomime to "asshole redneck culture." A sleazy stripclub, drag kings lining the gangplank, howling in macho delight as a trio of gaudy strippers parade obscenely by. The last temptress is portrayed by Divinity Fudge, a 300-pound black man in drag who the frenzied patrons attack in what Camille Paglia has coined "the giddy abandon of a gang rape." The third act, which reclaims violence as ritual by "taking from the wounds and giving to the audience," involves a series of deep cuts meticulously patterned on Divinity's back, whose blood is blotted onto paper, strung, sometimes over a hundred feet of clotheslines, and sent floating above the audience. Athey follows by performing a solo suicide scene, inserting sixteen large hypodermic needles in a geometric pattern up his arm and attacking his face with a needle the size of a stiletto, attempting to reclaim, through passion and ritual, the violations he has previously committed against himself in anger and frustration.

1997's *Deliverance* examined faith healing and the Filipino phenomenon of psychic surgery. On a stage covered in hundreds of pounds of dirt, three men on crutches come to see the Healer. They end up suspended on meat hooks to be bled while undergoing simulated surgical castration via genital stapling. Mummification and burial follows. Throughout the performance, a parade of images are employed, playing on themes culled from Santeria, Buddhism, Catholicism, and Judaism. Even Kali makes an appearance, interrupting a scene of double sodomy. In a light-hearted moment, the goddess severs the offending dildo in half with a pair of garden shears.

For the past five years, Athey has been focusing on *Joyce*, a multimedia theatrical presentation whose premise, like most of his previous work, summarizes the insane beliefs and outrageous behaviors of his family's religious perversity.

Raised in an extremely dysfunctional Pentecostal household, the young Ronnie Lee was sainted as a prophet messiah who proselytized in tongues, and whose tears were coveted by the entire congregation. The adoration bestowed upon him in the revival tent did little to alleviate the daily nightmares heaped upon him as an unwitting victim of his mother's schizophrenia, his aunt's hyper-sexualized insanity, and his grandmother's channeling of otherworldly specters.

Joyce debuted at the prestigious Kampnagel Theater in Hamburg, Germany in 2002. As Athey's most accomplished work, the stark beauty and emotional impact of this production all but defies description. Three immense screens project images of the young Athey self-mutilating, his aunt Vena undergoing an agonizing Betadine douche turned fist fuck for Jesus, his high-strung mother Joyce squirming and maniacally lint-picking, and his grandmother Annie Lou summoning the ectoplasmic angels whose beseeching shrill is exorcised in a series of automatic writing and action paintings.

The stage is platformed above the video screens and divided into four rooms where the main characters' repetitious compulsions escalate into an orgiastic frenzy. Mother Joyce, unable to withstand another moment of the voices within or the chaotic surround, smashes through the plasterboard walls while suspended upside down. Joyce has for the duration of the performance been trapped in a makeshift one-room insane asylum. The video screens vortex Joyce into infinity, an endless, unbelievably moving, visual spiral which reveals the vulnerability of body as prison.

Ron Athey forces the body to transcend its confines. His brilliance manifests as exorcism of, and for, the cauterizing of his own pain, and by pushing the boundaries of endurance through artistic expression, he shares his compassionate epiphany: We all need to break free from the shackles placed upon the individual by society, family, religion, and gender. And possibly through the catharsis of performance and ritual, we might finally be able to lay to rest the demons who've sent us in search of the respite only a knife or needle could at one time provide.

LL: How old were you when the spirit moved you to start preaching?

RA: Out of the four kids that were raised in our house, I was the only one that was interested in religion. My family didn't like churches . . . because they were too boring. At least they were right about something. We only liked revival meetings, so we were like church junkies in a way, going from revival tent to revival tent. Anywhere from the middle of the Mojave Desert, to Rosemead, to downtown Los Angeles. We lived in Pomona, about forty miles east of L.A. We were always on a journey—to see someone with stigmata, or someone who specialized in exorcisms. There was one church we went to where I felt like I could receive the gifts of the spirit . . . which is speaking in tongues. I was nine when it busted out of me.

LL: What busted out of you?

RA: The gloss-a-lalia! My own demons. I thought I was filled with something from outside of me. Something took over. I left my body. It was like being high. I was having an epileptic seizure while screaming at the top of my lungs.

LL: And you were being filled. That's the point of fevered religion.

RA: I still have it! I was a tiny, over-emotional, tender

creature and I remember being in this church. I started crying. So the minister took his white shirt off and tore it into squares, and put a tear on each square. And everyone lined up for one of my tears. So talk about grandiosity and self-importance! And the contrast of it . . . People were lining up for one of my tears. Meanwhile, I was going to an all-black school, in the poorest fucking neighborhood. My mother was in a mental institution and if I ever did anything wrong I was threatened to be put in a foster home. So it's like, *You're special, we love you!* and then, *You're about to LEAVE.*

LL: No special treatment at home for the little saint.

RA: Maybe compared to my brothers and sisters. My sisters had it worse. In creating *Joyce*, I wanted to show how sick it can be when women create a power structure. When they would bring my mother home from the institution, she would hear my sisters talking about her in the middle of the night and pull 'em out of bed by their hair. Out of bunk beds. CLUNK— on the concrete floor. My older sister was kind of good-looking, but she looked like someone threw her teeth at her from across the room. My grandmother would hold her by the chin and start slapping her face just for being ugly, until they both fell down. Really twisted shit. Instead of that sister being fucked up about her face, my younger sister went and had her entire face sawed apart then put back together. She had a half-inch of skull sawed out because you could see her gums when she smiled. She had a rib removed and her lower jaw extended.

LL: When did you decide body manipulation would become part of your artistic expression?

RA: I started self-mutilating at fifteen when I couldn't understand the concept of Jesus anymore. You're crying, and there's no one to pray to. I stuck tweezers in a light socket trying to wake my body up. I did cuttings with razor blades. Fingers, hands, arms. I would slam my head into concrete walls and floors. I felt like a numb piece of meat. That's when my head started ringing. I felt like I was just going to float away. Once I injured myself I would flatline a little bit so that I could go on with the next day.

LL: Is this when you began to ritualize the high of self-abuse?

RA: I think it's because I was exposed to S & M bars before the whole '70s thing was over. You'd go in and there'd be all these guys under the bar just drinking piss. Somebody in chaps is getting fucked in the ass. Someone with a hard-on getting strung up on a chain-link fence.

LL: And that made you feel right at home?

RA: I felt that's what I needed. Structure. I never wanted to belong. I was never a "boy" in that scene. I never joined it. But I would go there and get drunk and leave with someone or a couple people, get tied up, and be set on fire. We would run the whole gamut. I'd get shot up with homemade crank, feel like I had a stroke, then shit in some old man's mouth on a toilet seat on stilts. And there was NO LIMIT.

LL: When you first got into that scene before you understood the possibility of reclaiming your trauma and ritualizing it, did you feel any guilt over the transgressions you were committing?

RA: I had no guilt whatsoever. I wanted someone to

fucking kill me. And it felt good. I would go off with anyone and go anywhere. In the early '80s, I got into the Hitler Youth look. I remember going to bars and realizing that I had a different kind of power. Instead of someone sleeping with this weird boy all of a sudden, I was the top and someone was giving me a hundred bucks to kick him in the head with my boots on. I was experimenting and wide open to feeling everything. Somehow I had no taboos at all. I wasn't afraid of blood. I wasn't afraid of shit. I wasn't afraid of piss. I just walked into everything like a child, without any hangups. I have more hangups now than I had then.

LL: When did you stop using drugs?

RA: By the time I was twenty-five, I was dying. Too much heroin and methadone . . . and Valium. My first addiction. I was a trash bucket and I did so much LSD and crystal meth and speed when I was younger that I actually couldn't take any stimulant. If I did coke I'd be climbing the walls. Heroin was the end of the road for me. My nervous system was shot. Every time I'd do speed, I'd start hyperventilating the minute it hit my blood.

LL: How did you progress from sticking tweezers into electrical sockets, shitting in people's mouths, to body modification and performance?

RA: A lot of leather bars had piercing salons. The Gauntlet had opened in L.A. in the mid-'70s. Genital piercing in the back—my first encounter with expressing your freakishness through mutilation or adornment. When I was on acid, I would just take broken glass or tear a can open and cut myself. I wanted to feel blood pouring on me. And I would start cutting other people without asking. Here we are, twenty years later! *Joyce* was like pulling teeth for me. I had been writing notes on it for five years. The challenge was in making a work so personal about not only my schizophrenic mother but also three other schizophrenic women. And how it becomes one shared disease. All happening in an insane religious household where a twisted sexuality which revolves around red-hot Betadine douches and five long fingernails up the cunt is the daily order.

LL: You were only a child when this happened. Were you in the same room when this was going on?

RA: It happened in the bathroom at least once a week, during my whole life when I lived at home. The women in my family were obsessed by the idea that "you're filthy." And you probably are after a while because you don't have any natural enzymes left after you've rinsed yourself out, scrubbed yourself raw, and have had your mother jerk you off until you come, making you feel dirty and ashamed.

LL: When in reality the filth is coming from the victimizer who then drains you of your natural defense against their disease.

RA: Exactly the point. Performance as cleansing ritual from the disease of my mother.

AFTERWORD

SICK WITH DESIRE

I've always had an overwhelming compulsion to confess, to reveal the most revolting details of my existence to others. I possess a criminal predilection which bears no guilt yet admits to not only my own crimes of passion, but also my complicity in aggravating others to commit crimes both for and against me.

I play judge, jury, convict, and victim. A schizophrenic passion play that feeds on the intoxicating repercussions of the repetitive cycle of abuse. An unending theme in my body of work.

From my earliest lyrics, spoken word performances, and films, I have sung vicious incantations bemoaning the cruel fate of the human condition, where each of us bears some mark of battery.

We have all been victimized at some point because of our gender, race, age, socioeconomic status, religion, or lack of. Our first cry is slapped out of us as we are violently wrenched from the relative safety of the crimson universe deep within our mothers' bodies. Born in blood and battered into breathing, life begins with brutality and baptizes with violence.

And violence is an addictive electrical current which burns at both ends. Cruel lessons taught within the torture chamber of the nuclear family replayed with systematic repetition over and over again in our adult relationships until we are able to recognize the patterning of ritualized abuse and readdress our participation in its ongoing cycle.

I have always felt the need to strike back, not only at the closed fist of my father, our fathers, the fathers of our country and God—the father, that motherfucker—but at times, in a perverse reversal of roles, at parts of myself.

To attack my own body. To use my body as whipping post and sacrifice in submission to my own inherent sadomasochism. To that redneck faggot truck driver who overrides so many of the other sexual schizophrenics who cohabitate in this insane asylum, my body. Which is forever riddled by an agitation, an irritation, an insatiability. A need to be challenged, threatened, throttled, pushed to the brink—because anyone who has been traumatized by life realizes that to fully appreciate every breath, nothing short of fearing YOU WILL NOT BE ALLOWED TO TAKE ANOTHER ONE will renew your vigor for every moment that still remains.

My goal has always been to if not step off the wheel, away from the scaffold, and out from under the guillotine of genetically preprogrammed trauma bonds, to at least recognize that I am not the only one living under a life sentence of victimhood, willing or not. I am not the only one SICK WITH DESIRE.

I create as a form of public psychotherapy speaking to and for a minority of passionate extremists who feel either betrayed or never fully defined by gender.

I have always felt I was cross-dressing in my own flesh—a hotel for so many, many monsters.

And I admit it:
The American Way of Life has turned me into
A death-defying murder junkie
Drunk on disasters, calamities, casualties, bombs bursting in air, bullets ricocheting off the bellies of pregnant women, the bombing of abortion clinics, crippled children poisoned on a school bus, shopping-mall murders, crumbling cities polluted beyond repair, craters of despair in the eyes of men, women, and children, their brains rotted by the cathode glare of the television, the Internet, video games—

Where all the Killers are heroes
All the Killers are heroes . . .

And I myself am filled with a MURDEROUS RAGE
Gang Warfare waged under my skin
A battle of bitches boxing their way out

I have become the RAPIST whose IMPOTENCE
At annihilating the REAL KILLERS is MANIFESTED
As violence against myself
And anyone else who gets in my fucking way

A PASSION KILLER riddled with CRIMINAL URGES
A SADIST incarcerated in her own TORTURE CHAMBER
One minute you're FLESH AND BLOOD
And the next you're FLESH AND BONES
PILES AND PILES OF FLESH AND BONES

MY WAR IS THE BATTLE OF SEX AS AN ANIMAL ACT
FOUGHT HAND TO GLAND
ONE WOMAN VERSUS EVERY MAN

I've gotten inside the enemy's head
I'm sleeping in his fucking bed
MY WOMB—A TOMB—A SACRIFICIAL CUNT
THE MORE THEY KILL THE MORE I FUCK

Welcome to MY church—
The Church of the Unholy Redeemer
Where the only commandment is
REBELLION from FALSE VIRTUE
REBELLION from FALSE VIRTUE

Pleasure is the only true rebellion
Pleasure at the Mouth of the Abyss
Pleasure at the Brink of the Apocalypse
Ecstasy at the Brink of the Disaster

In Times of War—it's not my War—it's not your War
We, especially as women, need to insist upon our
      Pleasure
Demand our Pleasure
Because it's the first fucking thing they stole from us

And we might not have much Time left . . .
Small Pox, Anthrax, Avian Bird Flu, Nuclear Warheads
Biochemical Retribution as Revenge for Spiritual
      Bankruptcy
WE MIGHT NOT HAVE MUCH TIME LEFT

So with whatever Passion and Cruel Lucidity I can bring
to bear
I always wanted Life to be Naked
I always wanted Ecstasy and I finally found it
I must find Ecstasy in this Insanity
Freedom from their Slavery
The Truth in their Lies
Life in their Death
Beauty in their Homicidal Genocide
Peace in the War Whore's evil orgy of Death and
    Negation
Love amongst the Ruins
Pleasure in my own Pain

Also available from the Akashic Books

PARADOXIA: A PREDATOR'S DIARY
by Lydia Lunch
160 pages, trade paperback original, $13.95

"Hubert Selby, Jr. famously said that he grew up feeling like a scream without a mouth. Lydia Lunch, one of his most celebrated—and most uncompromising—literary progeny, delivered scream mouth, teeth, blood, hair, sperm, knife, and adrenaline . . ."
—Jerry Stahl, author of *Permanent Midnight*

"*Paradoxia* reveals that Lunch is at her best when she's at her worst . . . and gives voice to her sometimes scary, frequently funny, always canny, never sentimental siren song."
—Barbara Kruger, *ArtForum*

ISTANBUL NOIR
edited by Mustafa Ziyalan & Amy Spangler
300 pages, trade paperback original, $15.95

Brand new stories by: Lydia Lunch, Feryal Tilmaç, Rıza Kıraç, Hikmet Hükümenoğlu, Behçet Çelik, İsmail Güzelsoy, Jessica Lutz, Yasemin Aydınoğlu, Tarkan Barlas, Barış Müstecaplıoğlu, and more.

"Istanbul straddles the divide of Europe and Asia, and its polyglot population of twelve million seethes with political, religious and sexual tensions, as shown in the sixteen stories in this strong entry in Akashic's noir anthology series. Most of the stories are fittingly dark, though a couple are lit by a macabre humor . . . [A] welcome complement to the mostly historical mysteries set in Istanbul."
—*Publishers Weekly*

HIGH LIFE
by Matthew Stokoe
336 pages, trade paperback original, $15.95
*A selection of Dennis Cooper's Little House on the Bowery series

"*High Life* is perhaps the greatest neglected masterpiece of true noir. I've never read anything like this, nor do I expect to."
—Ken Bruen, author of *The Guards*

"Stokoe's in-your-face prose and raw, unnerving scenes give way to a skillfully plotted tale that will keep readers glued to the page."
—*Publishers Weekly*

INFINITY BLUES
poems by Ryan Adams
288 pages, trade paperback original, $15.95

"Ryan Adams, one of America's most consistently interesting singer/songwriters, has written a passionate, arresting, and entertaining book of verse. Fans are going to love it, and newcomers will be pleased and startled by his intensity and originality. The images are vivid and the voice is honest and powerful."
—Stephen King, author of *Duma Key*

GODLIKE
by Richard Hell
150 pages, trade paperback original, $13.95

Godlike, Hell's second novel, is a stunning achievement, and quite likely his most important work in any medium to date. Combining the grit, wit, and invention of *Go Now* with the charged lyricism and emotional implosiveness of his groundbreaking music, *Godlike* is brilliant in form as well as dazzling in its heart-wrenching tale of one whose values in life are the values of poetry. Set largely in the early '70s, but structured as a middle-aged poet's 1997 notebooks and drafts for a memoir-novel, the book recounts the story of a young man's affair with a remarkable teenage poet. *Godlike* is a novel of compelling originality and transcendent beauty.

SILENT PICTURES
photos by Pat Graham
144 pages, oversized paperback original w/color & b&w photos, $22.95

Modest Mouse, Ted Leo, Bikini Kill, Fugazi, and The Shins are just some of the subjects in acclaimed photographer Pat Graham's debut collection of work. The moments, the music, and the message all come alive with vivid intensity and searing honesty, as Graham documents the evolution of independent music history from his vantage point at the heart of the Washington, DC scene over the last two decades.

These books are available at local bookstores.
They can also be purchased online through www.akashicbooks.com.
To order by mail send a check or money order to:

AKASHIC BOOKS
PO Box 1456, New York, NY 10009
www.akashicbooks.com, info@akashicbooks.com

(Prices include shipping. Outside the U.S., add $8 to each book ordered.)